PORTENTS OF THE REAL

A Primer for Post-9/11 America

◆

SUSAN WILLIS

VERSO

London • New York

First published by Verso 2005
© Susan Willis 2005
All rights reserved

The moral rights of the author have been asserted

1 3 5 7 9 10 8 6 4 2

Verso
UK: 6 Meard Street, London W1F 0EG
USA: 180 Varick Street, New York, NY 10014–4606
www.versobooks.com

Verso is the imprint of New Left Books

ISBN 1–84467–023–6

British Library Cataloguing in Publication Data
A catalogue record for this book is available from the British Library

Library of Congress Cataloging-in-Publication Data
A catalog record for this book is available from the Library of Congress

Typeset in Garamond by Andrea Stimpson
Printed in the USA by R.R. Donnelley & Sons

For Fred

CONTENTS

INTRODUCTION

To celebrate Thanksgiving 2003, George Bush had himself secretly flown from his Texas ranch to Baghdad airport where he surprised the assembled troops with a Thanksgiving dinner. Like most American holidays, Thanksgiving is a celebration of the ideology of family. For us, the war in Iraq is represented in the media as a sundering of family – babies, spouses, and parents left at home while brave soldiers do their duty abroad.

The event was a stunning media coup for a President whose handlers certainly know how to produce images. If Ronald Reagan was known as the "Teflon" President for his bland, "no-stick surface" demeanor, George Bush is surely the digital President. Indeed, his entire career seems to have been filmed against the blue screen, essential to digitally produced superhero action figures. Where the Hulk leaps over mountains and Spiderman scales tall buildings, George Bush wades – Christ-like – through the expectant multitudes. In his arms, he bears neither sword nor loaves and fishes but a tray heavy with an oven-roasted turkey, decked with trimmings.

Like the President's dramatically staged landing on an aircraft carrier to announce the end of major hostilities in Iraq, Thanksgiving in Baghdad was meticulously choreographed. Start to finish, it was an elaborate photo op. Indeed, the turkey was a fake – a prop – a plastic bird. If Christ fed the hungry by producing abundance out of a single loaf and a handful of fishes, Bush presided over a mass feeding of packaged TV-dinner-style rations for the troops. And he presided over the mass deception of the multitudes at home, who saw the photos of the turkey – much like we saw the photos of Iraq's presumed weapons installations – and took sham for reality.

What did the President know and when did he know it? Did he poke at the bird on the tray and know it was fake? Did he feel the fool for responding to the soldiers' outstretched hands with a plastic meal? Or did he know he was already playing his part when he boarded Air Force One? (He had to have brought the plastic turkey with him.)

America lives its history as a cultural production. The post-9/11 era, as one defined by individual uncertainty in the face of an over-certain but often mistaken and repressive state, has seen a tremendous burgeoning of cultural forms meant to explain and manage the crisis. Daily life in America is articulated across an array of competing popular fictions. Perennial among these is the western. Here, we have a cowboy President, who hails from a ranch, has trouble with the finer points of language, and regularly practices the art of squinting into the sun. For swagger, the President has perfected a gait where the long stride of cowboy boots is cantilevered against the weight of a heavy belt buckle. To round out the scenario, we track our enemies with the aid of "Wanted Dead or Alive" notices, which we post, twenty-first-century style, on the "Rewards for Justice" website.

As the western moves from wide open spaces and into the frontier saloons and onto the Mississippi river boats, the genre expands to include gambling. Similarly, our post-9/11 cowboy story moved off the range and into the casino. As it did so, the "Wanted Dead or Alive" rhetoric morphed into the evildoers pack of cards. Thus, inscrutable Ba'athists were translated into the knowable and familiar as each of the high-ranking evildoers was assigned a specific suit and number. Saddam was, of course, the deadly Ace of Spades. Not surprisingly, and in line with a rigged game of poker, we eventually found our "ace in a hole." The pack of cards proved so successful amongst soldiers that hundreds of thousands of additional decks were quickly produced for sale in the US. However, most Americans did not use their cards for high-stakes poker. Rather, we played something more akin to "pick-up 52," a child's game in which the cards are merely tossed into the air leaving the player to reassemble and account for the entire deck. You win when you've got them all (55 in the case of the evildoer deck – jokers included).

The deck of cards wasn't the only way that the motif of gambling entered post-9/11 popular culture. The infamous department of governmental dirty tricks – DARPA, by acronym – proposed a far more adult game of chance. Trading futures in terrorism – what a terrific way to wed high-stakes gambling to contemporary high-risk finance! Brain child of John Poindexter, whose checkered past includes the Iran–Contra chicanery, players were supposed to place bets on future terrorist attacks. The level of the bidding would then determine the odds on favorites and indicate which dubious world figures were the most likely terrorist targets. According to Poindexter's twisted logic, more orthodox spy agencies would, then, know where to assign the spooks, protective forces, or undercover assassins. While public outcry quickly canceled Poindexter's lottery of death, the plan itself didn't die. Rather it relocated from the public sector to a private website, where we can currently play the terrorist options game while the government undoubtedly snoops on our bets.

True to the pliant nature of popular genres, the narrative of gambling quickly slides into spy movies. This was already apparent in the James Bond movies. However, contrary to Ian Fleming's rather elitist super spy, we in America can all be spies, democratically spying on each other. At least this was the aim of the various permutations of TIPS and TIA programs, both of whose acronyms promise "Total Information." Luckily, the majority of Americans balked at the idea of letter carriers and meter readers conveniently turning themselves into unofficial spies. Many of the plans for neighbors spying on neighbors were scrapped, their last vestige today inscribed in the huge highway signs across the interstates in the Washington DC area that urge motorists to "Report Suspicious Activity." What saved private citizens from the life of spying is redundancy. As with most forms of labor, technology has taken the place of hands-on – or eyes-on – activities. TIPS and TIA have been internalized, channeled into massive computerized data-mining systems that burrow tirelessly through the sum total of our collected data to assemble profiles based on the friends we keep, the languages we speak, the books we read – and, most certainly, our travel destinations. At this point, the spy thriller morphs into a sci-fi scenario, with retinal scans soon to be democratically required of everyone.

America is in popular genre hyperdrive, churning out formulaic fictions in a frenzied attempt to determine who we are and what we're doing. Our historical moment is like a cineplex where every genre is playing simultaneously. But popular culture is not a simple culture. We may gobble it up; but more often than not, we swallow difficult counter-meanings along with the predictable plots and characters. The following essays are exercises in recognizing that culture is always more than it seems. They are written in a language that captures the American vernacular. There are odd alliterations that suggest plays on meanings, words that pun or almost pun, ironic understatements, blatant quotidianisms, and downright quirky expressions. Buoyed by language, the reader swims in a cultural soup. But the discourse neither trivializes nor obfuscates. Rather, the vernacular unpacks the culture with the tools of the culture. For the most part, 9/11 has been told to us by outsiders looking in on us. Incisively, dramatically, provocatively, theorists such as Jean Baudrillard, Paul Virilio, and Slavoj Žižek filled the void of our silence. They articulated the meanings of our cataclysm while we struggled against widespread censorship. Our President made it clear that critical or contrary opinions would be deemed inappropriate. The mainstream media quickly adopted the party line. Only small left-leaning journals gave space to serious explorations of the meanings and implications of 9/11.

These essays appear harmless because they look at 9/11 through the oblique lens of culture. Moreover, each takes as its starting point an event or phenomenon that has either been trivialized or folded into formulaic explanations. The titles announce the vernacular and ground each study in the mundane. "Old Glory" considers mass patriotism under the rubric of our pet name for the flag. "Anthrax Я US" alludes to a popular chain of toy stores to address the anthrax hoaxes in the context of mass commodity consumption. "What Goes Around Comes Around" captures the logic of a folk truism to examine the Washington DC area snipers. "Only the Shadow Knows" mimics a radio drama from the '30s to suggest the essence of contemporary government secrecy. "The Greatest

Show on Earth" posits the circus to question the status of risk and risk-takers. And "Quien Es Mas Macho?" echoes the Spanglish commonly heard throughout the US to raise questions about centuries-old state-sanctioned violence.

Snipers, anthrax hoaxes, stuntmen, shadow government: be they trite or upsetting, all were perceived as random manifestations of everyday America. Yet, they came to us as portents – not separate from our greater historical reality, but embodying it and figuring it back to us. As surely as America avoids coming to grips with its history, that history emerges to haunt us, repeated across our culture as a series of figural representations. This book is a primer for how to read portents as heralds of our reality.

1

OLD GLORY

They just want to show their patriotism because that's all they can do.

A flag salesman in Durham NC interviewed on the BBC World Service (December 6, 2001)

In the wake of the attack on the World Trade Center, America responded with the rapid deployment of the American flag. The urge to display the flag was ignited by the Iwo Jima style image of the three firefighters who raised the flag over the rubble at the Lower Manhattan site and whose photograph was then emblazoned across the front pages of the nation's newspapers. Desire to perpetuate the heroic image has since impelled the development firm Forest City Ratner to commission a statue in the likeness of the photo which will be installed at the New York City Fire Department Headquarters. Subsequent calls that the statue reflect the multi-ethnic make-up of the victims of the attack – and America generally – have resulted in the decision to create a statue where two of the original white flag raisers will be replaced by representative black and Hispanic figures.

Many Americans who support the inclusion of non-white figures fail to realize that New York City's firefighters – like its police force – are almost exclusively white. Mayor Giuliani, everyone's hero of the day and *Time* magazine's "Man of the Year," reigned over this country's most ethnically diverse city with the most racially exclusionary uniformed brigades. The nation's desire to transform the statue of New York's firefighters into an emblem of diversity gives symbolic reversal to the city's racist policies. It also makes the statue a displaced icon of a different fighting force, which is racially diverse: the US military. In the guise of New York's firefighters the statue embodies the nation and facilitates a shift from the local to the international, from the work of recovery to the work of war. As a sliding signifier, the statue enables the nation's attention to move from Lower Manhattan to the new Iwo Jima in Kabul and Kandahar.

The desire to inculcate the statue with the spirit of multiculturalism also serves to assimilate America's non-white population under the flag of euphoria, in contradiction to the fact that the demonstrative display of flags has been a predominantly white response. Notwithstanding the Arab merchants who quickly attached the American flag to their homes and businesses in the hope of heading off attacks by rabid bands of US patriots, most black and Hispanic neighborhoods have been relatively flag free. Incorporating black and Hispanic figures into the composition of the firefighter's statue may well give recognition to the numbers of non-whites who serve the country, but its larger purpose is to launder the image of the flag itself and the country for which it stands – both better known by these same populations for sponsoring racial profiling, neighborhood sweeps by "la Migra," and doing everything possible to avoid reparations for slavery.

While the attitude of many non-white residents and citizens of the United States is one of letting white folks do their thing, the meanings attached to flag waving have a lot to tell us about the America that emerged phoenix-like out of its ashes to remake itself for the twenty-first century. This survey of flag scenarios looks beyond the various clichéd versions of "United We Stand" to consider ideologies implicit to empire and free market consumerism – all unfurled with the flag.

Not only is the flag displayed at fixed positions, on homes, freeway overpasses, and storefronts, it has also become a circulating signifier. The flag raised Iwo Jima style over New York's Ground Zero was subsequently shipped to Afghanistan where it was raised over the Kandahar airport. Passed from the hands of the firefighters to those of the Marines, the flag designates a shift in America's interests away from a host of domestic needs left pending after 9/11, and towards a politics aimed at military operations overseas, whose repercussion on the domestic is, then, the militarization of the homefront under the guise of Homeland Security. The fact that this particular flag can generate certain specific meanings in its New York incarnation and very different ones over Kandahar makes it a supersymbol. Indeed, in its power to evoke healing and perseverance over New York and retribution over Kandahar this flag shows itself as an empty signifier, capable of designating a host of referents without being perceived as contradictory. As empty signifier, this flag concentrates the power inherent in the commodity to become a fetish. Like the shroud of Turin, this flag speaks for a form of patriotism raised to the level of religion. As a physical object, it offers itself as relic – a replacement for a more properly materialist sense of history. As relic, it embodies the fundamentalism of the Bush White House where there is little distinction between ardent political conservatism and Christian evangelical values. One can imagine that the firefighter's flag will continue to circulate, following the anti-terrorist Special Forces brigade to all the world's hot spots. With each unfurling, the flag will consecrate yet another site crucial to America's efforts to secure the global production and distribution of oil. The existence of this flag will finally bestow meaning on all the flags we purchase at Wal-Mart and eBay. It proclaims the possibility of the unique object, the object that valorizes our investment of hopes and desires in our pitiful series of knock-offs.

Immediately following the collapse of the World Trade Center, with numbers of investment concerns in disarray and the economy spiraling into the recession nobody was willing yet to acknowledge, we were told to shop. Shop to show we're patriotic Americans. Shop to show our resilience over death and destruction. Shop because in consumer capitalism shopping is the only way we can participate. Contrary to our President's call to shop, many Americans chose, instead, to give blood as eucharistic bonding of our life and body with those stricken and maimed. The desire to make physical connection with others, to describe community in the exchange and circulation of blood, contrasts with the consumerist model of society where people are articulated as individual consumers rather than as members of a collectivity. While the donor model of community strikes a contrast, it is already being recycled into consumerism as a number of dystopian writers (Leslie Marmon Silko, for one) have begun to imagine a world where the poor are farmed for their organs, a situation become reality in China where wealthy consumers can bid on the organs of death-row inmates.

Americans overwhelmed blood donor sites even when it became apparent that the rubble would yield few survivors – indeed, few bodies. Awash in a sea of blood that couldn't possibly be used within the time that blood can be stored, blood banks urged donors to postpone their donations. The request that people delay the gratification associated with giving flies in the face of a nation trained to expect the sorts of gratifications associated with consumerism where pleasure is supposed to be spontaneous and continual. No wonder many turned to displays of the flag as the only available mode of proclaiming community. Remarkably, the great majority of Americans did not purchase a "real flag," one made of cloth to prescribed dimensions and typically hoisted up a flagpole, but chose instead to tape a paper version on their car window or mount a plastic one on their car antenna. Did they anticipate that the flag craze would undergo the obsolescence of all commodities, making the paper or plastic flag most appropriate? Or did they intuit that in a society wholly defined by consumerism plastic is most representative; indeed, there can be no real object (except the super-fetish circling the globe with the Special Forces). Finally, the display of flags underscores the importance of quantity over quality. Engulfed and smothered in flags, we consume them visually. Much of the American landscape gives the impression that we all shopped at a Wal-Mart where the only item on the shelf is the flag.

While the flag is an empty signifier, the context of its display endows it with meaning. For instance, flags displayed in the Garden District of New Orleans, all of them cloth and flagpole appropriate, absorb the meanings generated by their ambient context defined by upper-middle-class comfort and good taste. The trolley ride down St. Charles Street evokes a journey down Embassy Row, with every embassy flying the same flag. As testament to America's global reach, the view down St. Charles Street bespeaks America's new alliances in the fight against terrorism, wherein every nation's own troublesome dissidents become a pretext to adopt America's search-and-destroy policy: Russia's war against the Chechens, China's repression of its Muslim population in Xinjiang province, and Israel's drive to exterminate the Palestinians – all implicitly fly the American flag of approval.

Many Americans in more humble districts and abodes not nearly so grand as the mansions of the Garden District have refrained from the hubris of mounting a disproportionately huge flag on the front porch and instead chosen to incorporate a flag in the larger landscape setting of the house. Flags can be seen sprouting from garden beds and hanging from trees – both sites probably frowned upon by the guardians of flag etiquette. Of the flags displayed in gardens, the great majority are intimately connected with the homeowner's mailbox. Draped round the mailbox post, attached to the red mailbox "flag," or popping out of the ground next to the mailbox, the flag and mailbox declare a symbiotic relationship that bespeaks the nation's political unconscious. In connecting flag to mailbox, we give symbolic recognition to the dead and endangered postal workers whose exposure to anthrax was belatedly and inadequately addressed by the self-same government that claims to act in the name of the flag. In contrast to the employees of the Hart Senate Office building, who were carefully screened for anthrax, their offices under-going costly and lengthy fumigation, postal workers were summarily overlooked even though it was obvious that the mail that brought anthrax to Senator Daschle's office passed through the hands and buildings of postal workers. In turning our mailboxes into flag shrines, we acknowledge that our country treats its workers unequally and we make symbolic gesture to restore parity by giving recognition to those who otherwise died disregarded and in vain.

By far the most preferred site for flag display is the automobile. Taped to the inside rear window, tattooed into the paint, or streaming from tailgate or antenna, the auto flag makes every roadway into a Fourth of July parade route. Flags on cars can give rise to patriotic forms of road rage as the drivers of noticeably flag-bedecked autos attempt to cut off drivers deemed less patriotic by the telltale absence of a car flag. A passive-aggressive form of road rage is manifested by the pick-up truck convoy, traveling at 10mph and forcing a long line of motorists to queue up begrudgingly. The various forms of flag-induced road rage bespeak the ideological blackmail – brought to bear not only on America's allies but on all of us as well – of the slogan "If you're not with us, you're against us."

In the days immediately following 9/11, many Americans in places far removed from Ground Zero took to the roads in a frustrated attempt to get away from the twenty-four-hour news coverage and in search of other shell-shocked Americans. Since we are held together by our interstates and conduct much of our daily lives from behind the wheel of our cars, it's not odd that we would take to our cars in the effort to connect. With public transport at a halt, the private car was our only access to the freedom of mobility. The foray out on the road was apt to dramatize all the socially symbolic meanings we attach to cars generally – and by extension to the flags they fly. Predictably, the biggest, most numerous, and most noticeable flags are mounted on pick-ups and SUVs. Even while radio and TV pundits continue to disclaim the feeble voices from the left that suggest a link between the removal of the Taliban and their questionable efficacy as stewards of the trans-Uzbek pipeline, we Americans show with our car-mounted flags that we know the war against terrorism is the code term for the preservation of our interstates, cars, suburbs, and the petro-chemical octopus that feeds and clothes us.

While all our displays of the flag partake of ritual practices and meanings (if only in the way we mount our flags and later decide when it's appropriate to take one down), there is one use of the flag that far outstrips all others for ritual import. This involves the six thousand flags – most probably diminutive – reported to have been blasted into space with American astronauts aboard space shuttle Endeavour. The astronauts also brought aboard three large flags, one from the World Trade Center, another from the Pentagon, and the third from the Pennsylvania State Capital, in an effort to consecrate these for more earthly missions. The number of small flags was meant to symbolize the then purported six thousand victims of the attack on the World Trade Center. That the number of victims has now been scaled back to half the original estimate means that we now have a surplus of ritually charged flags. Rather than being freighted into space and jettisoned into the heavens where they might ritualize our nation's release from the stubborn pursuit of body parts and DNA molecules at Ground Zero, these flags were destined to return to earth, bearing with them the persistent dead weight of America's obdurate responsibility to physically account for each and every victim. We saw some of the same grim determination in the desperate attempt to recover the bodies buried under hundreds of feet of water off the coast of Nova Scotia, lost when Swissair flight 111 plummeted into the sea. Why this mania to recover the physical remains of loved ones lost in catastrophe, particularly when what's left is apt to be unrecognizable if not grisly?

Perhaps we are driven by the tantalizing possibilities offered by our own technologies. We seek the blood stains because we can actually make a positive identification with molecular evidence. We are a nation enthralled with forensics for whom Ground Zero offers a real-life stage equal to TV's new hit drama *Crime Scene Investigation*. Does it matter that the funds earmarked to bring DNA testing to bear on the convictions of many of our nation's death-row inmates have been diverted to Ground Zero? Clearly, some lives – or deaths – count more than others, particularly when it comes to accountability at Ground Zero where large insurance-premium holders have more death capital than those who will receive government compensation alone. On a larger scale, looking beyond inmates and victims, Americans generally count more than the world's others. The value of the handful of American deaths occasioned by the bombing of Afghanistan – calculated as each was brought home for televised memorials – far outweighs Afghanistan's estimated four thousand civilian deaths which do not compute in the   calculus of US television coverage. These faceless, nameless non-victims have the negative value comparable to a Third World nation's IMF debt.

Ever since the Oklahoma City bombing, our media have harped on about our nation's need to find "closure." In the case of the Murrah Federal Building, closure could only be obtained once we found, buried, and memorialized each and every victim; and then finalized our mourning with Timothy McVeigh's execution. The quest for closure became media fodder, filling the twenty-four-hour news networks and perpetuating our need to achieve – possibly document – what amounts to a collective psychic event based on a collective bookkeeping. The accountability of death puts mourning on a balance sheet where closure indicates an account paid. What about an unbalanced equation? Or, possibly, an open account? What about the fiscal uncertainty that really defines our lives and typifies the exponential growth of capital as a system based on speculation where bankruptcy is a fact of life? Fanatically craving closure, we attempt to bring accountability into our daily lives as a futile counterbalance to a system that shreds accountability like an Enron balance sheet. What's lost in the desperate desire for closure as a corrective to chaos is the possibility of imagining death as an open ending, as a disappearance that absolves the living from possessive attachment.

In our unwillingness to simply let the dead disappear, we express a deep cultural antipathy for ambiguity. We are living in a time of obdurate literal mindedness that can't tolerate anything that smacks of a symbolic disappearance. Like the insurance companies that detected false 9/11 claims, we police death with the demand for proof. Just as our dead must be accounted for;

so too must Osama bin Laden be found "dead or alive." We find it intolerably frustrating that the object of our military manhunt eludes capture even while his video image keeps appearing on an upstart non-western television station. In the same way that we excavate the rubble of the World Trade Center, sifting the debris for bloodstains and body parts, we search the caves of Tora Bora for Al Qaeda stragglers. A culture incapable of experiencing disappearance as cleansing release, a culture whose passion is reduced to the literal has become the epitome of the fundamentalism for which we condemn the Taliban.

The flags transported into space and conveyed back to earth are meant to be given to the families of the 9/11 attack. Leaving aside the American hubris that assumes every victim's family will want an American flag, including the families of foreign nationals and those of the illegal immigrants thought to have been in the World Trade Center's subterranean basements, the space flags bespeak an allegory for the twenty-first century, wherein religion merges with science and technology. Transported into space, the flags were literally brought closer to God. Have we devolved to the level of the child who imagines God in his heavenly throne amongst the clouds? Or do we imagine that the flags, like the space tourist Dennis Tito, were launched into the ultimate trip and meant to imbibe the essence of America's technological and scientific know-how as counterweight to the Russian know-how that Tito imbibed? By reason of their ritual journey, the space flags resolve contradiction. Consecrated, they return to earth bearing religious and technological benediction.

The distribution of the space flags amongst the victims' families commemorates the federalization of 9/11. Employees of private enterprise have become with their deaths America's war heroes. Their transformation from private to public employees renders their families the beneficiaries of Federal compensation. While precedents for Federal compensation can be found in government payments to the victims of natural disasters such as floods, fires, and earthquakes, the federalization of the World Trade Center has the political benefit of nationalizing the event, which in turn provides a convenient rationale for America's undeclared war. With three thousand individuals who died for our country, who among us felt justified in taking a strong stand against the bombing of Afghanistan? Witness the contortions amongst the editors and writers of the *Nation*, our country's most widely distributed left-liberal newspaper, that promulgated the dubious category of a "just war." Moreover, with the government offering Federal compensation, who among the victims' families will choose to forgo the sure and easy payment for the sake of launching a risky private suit? With its mass tort the government buys silence. It pays to eliminate the possibility of thousands of private suits that may not have garnered the claimants more money but would have uncovered possible areas of blame in the private sector.

Notwithstanding the secret CIA headquarters in the World Trade Center complex, the great majority of the victims died in the service of global finance capital. Like the thousands who lost their jobs and pensions because they staked their futures on Enron, the victims of the World Trade Center staked their futures on enterprises targeted because they are synonymous with our country's commitment to global capitalism. To raise a private suit is to demand that big business be deemed accountable.

Less grandiose than the space flags and more personal than the mailbox and car flags are the flags we sport on our T-shirts. Emblazoned across our chests, the flag becomes one with the rock bands and sports teams that also claim our allegiance and warrant a T-shirt's stamp of approval. The nation that condemns flag desecration shows no qualms over making the flag into a fashion statement. This is because the dictates of a society built on consumerism are supported by the Bill of Rights, where the individual's guarantee of freedom of speech has been extended to corporations as individual entities whose speech acts included, until recently, soft-money political contributions as well as T-shirt logos.

With flags on our shirts, we express the heartfelt desire to contribute our individual pledge to the collective endeavor even while we simultaneously recognize that the American endeavor is to consume commodities and ensure their worldwide distribution. In the wake of 9/11, many T-shirt ads emphasized that the shirt on sale was "made in America." Would it matter if our flag T-shirts were screen printed in Haitian sweatshops given the fact that many "official" Disney products come from such places, where they are sometimes made by children who are the age mates of the American children who wear Disney paraphernalia? For its triviality the T-shirt flag concretizes the global circulation of the commodity. It is the mundane emblem for the welding of market capital to empire. Finally, all over the world we can all buy America even though the day is fast approaching when nothing will be made in America. No matter, all the world's citizens will be able to trade in our logos. Our friends and allies may find it "cool" to wear our flag, while our enemies will find it in the litter of their countries' war zones – stamped on the mine, bomb, and grenade fragments as indication that retribution is also made in America.

2

ANTHRAX Я US

In the wake of 9/11, when the nation was still reeling from the attacks on the World Trade Center, the Pentagon and the media, apparently unsatisfied with the disaster at hand, began disseminating the fear that terrorists, having succeeded in shutting down air travel and the stock market, might launch a follow up attack using chemical or biological weapons. Whether prescient or causal, TV and radio journalists were soon to see their fears realized in a wave of anthrax mailings, five of them real and tens of thousands of them hoaxes. Conveyed on the waves of hysteria over anthrax, the impact of the terrorists' incursion spread to the far corners of the country – the west coast, the south, the rural, the suburban, places that otherwise reckoned themselves low on the terrorists' list of potential targets. The shock waves unleashed by the airplanes that slammed into our nation's economic and military centers were displaced into vectors of biological attack, both real and imaginary. These fanned out and penetrated the most mundane recesses of hometown America. College mailrooms began quarantining cookies from home; tons of mail, including batches of SAT exams, were sealed and stockpiled for future anthrax testing; numbers of commercial flights were redirected and forced to land when white powder (invariably Sweet and Low) was discovered on tray tables. The trivial stuff of daily life – vanilla pudding mix, powdered sugar, flour, talcum powder – suddenly had the power to close schools, cancel the mail, shut factories, and otherwise halt business-as-usual.

The country was in a panic. White powder was turning up everywhere. Citizens were afraid to receive, much less open their mail. Government agencies, the Postal Service, and the Centers for Disease Control were slow to issue precautionary advice. And when advice came, it seemed to heighten the public's anxiety. We were told to look for suspicious letters: no return address, curious combinations of postage stamps, downward slanting printing, inexplicable bulk, an unexpected package, and above all: white powder. We were told to seal the suspicious letter in a plastic bag, likewise our clothes, and shower immediately. With the advice came hundreds more hoaxes and hundreds more false alarms. People began demanding and stockpiling Cipro, the antibiotic of choice. Some, who were never exposed, began dosing themselves in advance even though doctors warned that the drug carried undesirable side effects.

Paranoia reached its apex with reports of real anthrax deaths. Some of the mortally stricken – the journalist for *Sun News* in Florida, the postal worker in New Jersey – seemed somehow more explicably in the terrorists' loop. Members of the media were clearly targets, although *Sun News* hardly ranks in importance with NBC. Postal workers were secondary targets brought into the terrorists' plot because the mail was the medium of delivery to primary targets like Senator Daschle's Office. We rationalized their deaths while we plotted our distance from government, the media, and the centers where mail is sorted. We relived the experience of children in the Cold War who computed the distance of their homes and schools from likely targets of nuclear attack. Some of us bought gas masks for ourselves and family members even though expert opinion held that anthrax spores could easily penetrate the mask's filter. All our strategies to create a false sense of security collapsed when Kathy Nguyen, a hospital worker in New York, and Ottilie Lundgren, an elderly woman in rural Connecticut, both died of inhalation anthrax. Where were they on our imaginary maps of proximity to terror? By what convoluted logic might we connect their deaths to the targets we deemed intentional and thereby know that we didn't share their fatal connection?

In an effort to take control of the mounting hysteria, President Bush warned that anthrax pranks would constitute a "serious criminal offense."[1] Hoaxers were threatened with a felony conviction under the legal rubric that penalizes for falsely reporting a fire or explosion. Even the threat of seven years incarceration did not quell the hoaxers, although it did cause one to take flight: a father who fled with his young son, abandoned his house, and disappeared, after sprinkling white powder in his ex-wife's office. Reportedly, the wife was more distraught over the disappearance of her child than the powdery office.[2]

Throughout the plethora of anthrax hoaxes from late September to mid-December, there was a fundamental dislocation between the serious threat of felony conviction and the pranksterism that informed the great majority of anthrax hoaxes. While some hoaxes were sent to settle a grudge – another ex-husband sent one to his wife's attorney and a Cook County prosecutor hoaxed a fellow prosecutor[3] – many hoaxes concluded with a smiley face or the words HA HA HA![4] Maybe the perpetrators were fed up with the culture of "Have a Nice Day" and gave expression to an undetected and unacknow-ledged dark side of a society that otherwise puts on the glossy smiley face of consumption. Bear in mind that this was the period when the stock market plummeted and we were being told to buy, buy, buy to save America. Among the pranksters not thrown out of work by the collapsing economy and the blow to the airline and vacation industries were a fair number who simply wanted to cancel work. These risked the threat of felony conviction to shut down packing houses and warehouses – even a General Motors assembly line where three workers attached an envelope containing the obligatory white powder and a note scrawled in their version of Arabic script to the windshield of a car as it moved down the line.[5] At a more junior level, but also motivated by the desire to avoid work, great numbers of middle- and high-schoolers across the country perpetrated anthrax hoaxes in the hopes of being dismissed early or being excused from homework. Having saturated the young and old prankster communities in the United States, anthrax hoaxes began to be reported all over the world. Not surprisingly, our allies the British had already experienced more than five hundred anthrax scares in London alone by the third week in October 2001.[6] Much like the globalization of the free market, anthrax scares cropped up in more remote places: Nairobi, Kenya; Amman, Jordan; and not to be outdone, our newest ally, Pakistan, had its quota of hoaxes. Is it possible that the fear of being perceived as "against us" in our war on terrorism provoked these far flung places to manifest a sympathetic display of the symptoms that define our hysteria? Desperately wishing to be counted "with us" they adopted our phobias.

In the general paranoia of fall 2001, many Americans failed to realize that the anthrax hoax was not born with 9/11 or even with the letter that contaminated Senator Daschle's Office. The Gulf War in 1991 ignited the concern over weapons of mass destruction and the fear that Saddam Hussein had been testing anthrax as one component of his larger arsenal. When photos from space revealed Iraqi fields strewn with dead animals we were sure they had been the victims of biological warfare. Throughout the '90s, anthrax was on peoples' minds but remained somewhat dormant until April 24, 1997 when a petri dish labeled "anthrachs" (sic) was sent to the Washington DC offices of the B'nai B'rith. The dish contained a gooey red substance, later proven to be harmless.[7] The hoaxer culture had not yet discovered that the preferred medium of delivery is white powder, but it very quickly realized that pseudo anthrax can wreak havoc. In the case of the B'nai B'rith, employees and police who walked through the "hot zone" had to remove their clothes, take showers, and undergo quarantine in a local hotel.

By 1999, anthrax had become the hoax of choice, far surpassing bomb threats with more than a hoax a day called into the FBI. Part of its popularity may have to do with the hoaxee's need to strip, shower, and submit to quarantine. Imagine the perverse thrill of emptying a busy department store and causing shoppers and employees alike to trot through an outdoor shower. Does the prankster watch from a nearby window or see it all on the local TV news? Perhaps the most devastating pre-9/11 hoax occurred at a Planned Parenthood facility in Kansas City, Missouri when an anthrax threat caused twenty people to endure an outdoor shower in the midst of a snow storm and freezing temperatures.[8]

Planned Parenthood has long born the brunt of anthrax hoaxes far more sinister than prankish. Remarkably, the government gave little attention to its plight, perhaps reluctant to infringe the speech rights of anti-abortionists who have secured the right to girdle abortion clinics with their pickets and heckle employees and clients alike. Only after 9/11 with real and false anthrax causing nationwide consternation did Federal Marshalls arrest Clayton Lee Waagner, self-proclaimed member of the "Army of God" and guilty of more than 550 admitted anthrax threats against abortion providers. Apparently, Waagner Fed-Exed his threats and charged his letters to Planned Parenthood's mail code. The consummate narcissist, Waagner was apprehended at a Kinko's store, busily surfing the web for headlines and news tidbits about himself. While Attorney General John Ashcroft praised the Kinko's employee who tipped Federal Marshalls of Waagner's whereabouts, Ashcroft had earlier betrayed his more complicated emotions regarding the hoaxes in a statement issued before Waagner's arrest. Vowing to apprehend and prosecute the perpetrators of anthrax hoaxes, Ashcroft proclaimed "They create illegitimate alarm in a time of legitimate concern."[9] Did the Attorney General mean to imply that our experience of alarm might be illegitimate? Or was he pondering the legitimacy of the Army of God as opposed to our country's own God fearing Army?

If the Attorney General included Freud along with his daily Bible readings, he might recognize anthrax as the return of the repressed. Indeed, it is the oldest identified pestilence known to medical science. Moses may well have been the first to use the disease as a bioweapon. Hugh Pennington quotes the book of

Exodus to prove the point: Apparently, the Lord told Moses to "'sprinkle ashes toward the heaven in the sight of Pharaoh'." When he did so "the ashes 'became a boil breaking forth with blains upon man, and upon beast'."[10] In Roman times, anthrax decimated flocks throughout the Mediterranean. More recently, it has been the object of experiments launched by the Nazis, the KGB, and our own military establishment. Bacillus anthracis, one of the simplest of life forms, traverses the centuries with the promise of microbial apocalypse. Here we thought we had put the old scourges behind us, banished the plagues with the Middle Ages. We imagined we had entered a whole new world of cleaner, more abstract viral agents of destruction, those codes that attach themselves to e-mail in the same way they attach themselves to DNA to cause system-wide failure. HIV is just as deadly as anthrax, but slower and far more complicated. It's a disease worthy of a society that has progressed from splitting atoms to splitting and modifying the genes. By comparison, anthrax is simple and quick. Conveyed by spores, it kills like the agents of an alien invasion in a B science-fiction movie from the '50s. So here we are at the dawn of the twenty-first century confronted by the threat of extermination by a simple bacterium, plunged by a pre-modern scourge into a postmodern plague hysteria. Clearly, with the mail identified as the vector of contamination, we best use e-mail where the risk is to our computer rather than ourselves.

As the repressed matter of a supposedly bygone era, anthrax haunts the subsurface of our glossy and suburbanized present.

Identified in the nineteenth century as wool-sorters' disease, it has migrated out of the industrial mill to become the disease of letter sorters. Not coincidentally, some of the hoaxers are postal workers; one among them, Clarence Lindsey, who scrawled "Anthrax Inclosed"[11] (sic) on a package at his job site. Known in Britain throughout the nineteenth century as an occupational disease, it affected "butchers, slaughtermen, dock labourers, fellmongers, hair curlers, carpet makers, brush makers, keepers in zoos and tanners."[12] Today's mad anthraxer may well be a biotech version of Timothy McVeigh rather than an underling of Saddam Hussein. Indeed, right-wing militia groups have for years circulated books and pamphlets such as "Biology for Aryans," "Biotoxic Weapons," and "Advanced Biological Weapons Design and Manufacture." These "how to" books promote the use of biological agents over bombs for their lethal toxicity and fear factor.[13] The Bush administration's rabid quest for WMDs in Iraq rendered our own biological terror industry largely invisible. In mimicking the real anthrax mailings, thousands of hoaxers gave symbolic expression to our society's best kept secret: the biggest repository of weapons of mass destruction turns out to be the United States not Iraq. The truth of the hoaxes is that anthrax, unlike the great majority of our consumables, is truly "Made in America." If anthrax represents the return of the repressed, it's not the history of humankind's struggle against a natural scourge that comes back to bedevil us, but the clandestine, top-secret production of weapons grade bacteria in our own laboratories.

Anthrax mobilizes and combines two types of public health fears. On one side of the equation is the fear of mass poisoning; on the other, the dread of pollution. Poison has typically been the weapon of the disadvantaged and the oppressed. Most effectively used by the slaves of Santo Domingo who used their knowledge of local herbs to distill venomous elixirs, poison was an instrument of rebellion. Long before Toussaint organized a slave army, poison wreaked havoc amongst the plantation owners whose slaves dosed their food and water with fatal draughts. More recently and in a lighter vein, poison permeates a number of popular fiction genres. As the weapon of stealth, the weapon of the weak, it is favored by women in romantic melodramas, spies in cloak-and-dagger fiction, and genteel murderers in British whodunits.

Notwithstanding its popular fiction associations, poison is also a fact of industrial life where it runs the gamut from the petro-chemical solvents we absorb through our skin to the lead we inhale and ingest. Industrial toxins contaminate our air, water, and soil. No longer the isolated agent – the cyanide pill or the strychnine-laced dessert – poison is part and parcel of industrial pollution. Indeed, pollution is poison in ambient form. It's the lead-based paint in older houses, the PCB's in the Hudson, and the plume of toxic particles that rose over Lower Manhattan to mark Ground Zero. While anthrax threatened employees in Tom Brokaw's New York office, hundreds of thousands of New Yorkers – from clean-up crews to ordinary residents – breathed the toxin-laden air that befouled the city

for months after 9/11. Oddly, the great majority of New
Yorkers did not choose to leave the city, although many were
without work, during the weeks of dense air pollution. Those
whose apartments were in the immediate vicinity of the
World Trade Center were relocated to hotels, otherwise close
to vacant due to the slump in the tourism industry. Controversy
would later rage over the Environmental Protection Agency's
monitoring of the so-called plume, particularly regarding the
Agency's mid-November 2001 announcement that the plume
no longer posed a public health hazard. Residents who had left
Lower Manhattan were told to return to their apartments only
to discover some four months later that the air over New York
still harbored dangerous levels of toxic particles, a mixture of
lead, asbestos, fiberglass, and mercury. The apparent split at the
EPA, with administrators countermanding the evidence of the
monitors, coincided with pressures from an insurance industry
no longer willing to foot the bill for all those lengthy hotel
stays. Is it any wonder that one of those accused of issuing a
false anthrax threat was a state environmental protection
worker?[14]

The sinister diffusion of anthrax hoaxes intersects with
our more common everyday worries over pollution. The
environmental protection worker's false threat articulates the
implicit connection between anthrax and anthracite, making the
disease an analog for coal in bacterial form. Taking its name
from the black carbuncle that can form on the skin of an
infected individual, anthrax is called "charbon" in French,

which also means coal. While we do not all live and breath under Manhattan's toxic plume, we do all suffer the fallout from the coal industry. The dreaded disease of generations of coal miners, black lung, is one variant of "charbon" poisoning for which Manhattan anthrax is the metaphorical biological equivalent. The thousands of anthrax hoaxes (by mid-December 2001 the Postal Service had received 15,800)[15] menace us with the horror of airborne spores, not unlike the coal-fired particulate pollution responsible for numerous respiratory diseases including asthma and lung cancer. Not all of us have received an anthrax hoax in the mail, but we daily reap the rewards of "charbon" in our acid rain and greenhouse gasses. Anthrax encapsulates the truth of a society bent on progress and sacrificing itself to industry. As metaphor for pollution, the anthrax hoax gives the lie to everything our economy holds dear.

As cryptogram for our own bioterrorism industry and metaphor for our own choking industrial pollution, anthrax is US, our most appropriate logo. It might well be the brand name for a commodity more widely known than the heavy metal band that dubbed itself "Anthrax." In the world of commodity capitalism where much of daily life is played back to us in a flow of images, Guy Debord's definition of the spectacle is a truism. In the context of a society bemused by its own spectacle, the hoax event functions counter-intuitively as the truth that unmasks the lie that we take for reality. In dramatic contestation of John Ashcroft, who saw the false anthrax threats as provoking "illegitimate alarm," the hoax may be one of the few events capable of eliciting real feelings in a culture that lives the pseudo reality of the commodity. Even the destruction of the Twin Towers has been absorbed into spectacle, played back to us in replicate and re-memorialized for media diffusion at every possible occasion. In a surfeit of the real become image, the hoax, as untruth, bursts asunder the complacency of daily life. It jolts us out of our anomie and begs us wonder why so many law-abiding citizens chose to break the law with a prank.

Surely we are not dissatisfied? Aren't we the nation of the well supplied, so far from want that we will soon be dying of obesity? Aren't we the nation whose contentment manifested itself in the aftermath of 9/11 with a whopping 90 percent presidential approval rating? Could it be that the anthrax hoaxes belie unacknowledged discontent, the repressed dark humor of dissatisfaction?

Just as we've come to acknowledge the hollow gratification of the commodity — how lackluster it appears once we've brought it home and unwrapped it — so too might we recognize the tarnished nature of our President, appointed by Supreme Court fiat. Just as the commodity is a sham, so too might we see our president, scripting himself, along with his Shadow Government, in a remake of *Dr. Strangelove*. Commenting on the "fraud of satisfaction,"[16] Debord points to an endless cycle of consumption, with each new commodity meant to overcome the dissatisfaction of the previous one. Similarly, we look ahead to a new election cycle, attempting to trick our despair with newly passed campaign finance reform and redrawn precinct maps. In the political economy of consumer dissatisfaction, the hoax functions as a negation. It intervenes in a cycle of commodity-fueled desires whose penetration of the political reveals itself in our President's popularity polls and photo ops in elementary schools. The hoax is the negative event that disrupts business-as-usual. The hoax summons the forces of the system to derail the system. The hoax cannot imagine a new political order, but it impedes the one that exists.

The hoax is a symbolic ploy that takes aim at the spectacular. It is the unreal bent on conjuring the real. It gives disaffected individuals tremendous power over similarly disaffected individuals. Most dramatically, it summons the police, biohazard specialists, truckloads of equipment, the media; and it throws everyone out of the ordinary and into a new hard-edged, life-and-death reality. It fractures time, disrupts the boring linearity of time on the job or at school, all those hours that we add up and translate into pay checks and taxes – what Debord calls the "infinite accumulation of equivalent intervals."[17] Like a monkey wrench thrust in the cogs of the daily grind, the hoax ruptures commodified time. Its product is the non-product of delay. Time is money, whether on the job or on vacation. We make, we spend. The hoax interjects the negative temporality of lost time. It creates hiatus, an oasis of anti-temporality in the tyranny of linear time. Is it any wonder that many judges have fined anthrax hoaxers the monetary equivalent of the time lost due to their prank? Such rulings suggest that our system can't abide the absence of production and must levy fines as compensatory earnings.

BUT IT'S ALL A HOAX, a choreographed event. As performance, the hoax translates our real experience into the hyper-real. According to Jean Baudrillard, simulation exists to lend credence to the real.[18] For him, Disneyland exists only so the rest of LA might appear to be its antithetical truth. However, the subtlety of simulation is that neither Los Angeles, volatile home of heartbreak and illusion, nor Disneyland, playground of themed desires, is real. Similarly, real and pseudo anthrax infuse each other with meaning. The hoax is produced as if it were real, and the real is produced by the media as spectacle. Indeed, the media requires the difference – albeit indistinguishable except in outcomes – between the real portrayed as spectacle and the hoax lived as real – both locked in a spectral replication that undermines the reality of both terms. It is significant that in the long list of anthrax hoaxers there are no TV or radio newscasters. Their absence from the ranks of the hoaxers speaks for the conflation of entertainment and news made banal with the assimilation of the networks to leisure industry giants like Disney. The government's decision to cancel its plans for an "Office of Strategic Information," meant to disseminate various shades of falsehood everywhere but in the United States, merely eliminates a redundancy. In a society incapable of distinguishing dis-, mis-, and real information, the hoax serves as alibi for what we take as real.

What's most real about the anthrax hoaxes is the way the vast majority of Americans failed to see them as pranks. Under the pall of terror, we canceled comedy. Minutes before the attacks, we were laughing along with Molly Ivins over our President's malapropisms. Seconds later, we became grimly straight-laced. Gone were satire, the mainstay of left and liberal criticism; and irony, commonplace of the postmodern condition; even sarcasm, bitter pill of the post-punk generation. In their place were trauma, intensified and perpetuated by an obsessive media dwelling on its own images of woe; and fundamentalism, a culture-wide, narrow-minded adhesion to the most literal interpretation of all things. Patriotism became the cure for trauma and the demonstration of fundamentalism. Like patients in a mental ward, we were swaddled and bound by a patriotism so omnipresent it verged on fascism. Told to mind our tongues, thoughts, and acts, we embraced military bombardment in Afghanistan and Homeland Security.

This was the climate that gave birth to the anthrax hoaxes. With all avenues to humor foreclosed, dreadful but innocent white powder began appearing on desktops and doorknobs. A rumor, a whisper, a doubt, it sifted out of our mail even while we enthusiastically waved our flags. In a climate of fundamentalism where criticism is equated with terrorism and all forms of terror are equally absolute, we failed to grasp the prank as symbolic act. Lost was the possibility of seeing in the prank all the petty and profound dissatisfactions that inform daily life. Never heeded were the intuitive ways that the prank seized and prized open our culture's most basic meanings. In the aftermath of 9/11, we missed the chance to read the prank's counter-meanings.

Having succumbed to fear, we chose not to fly …

3

WHAT GOES AROUND COMES AROUND

The month following our nation's commemoration of the thousands who died in the attacks on the World Trade Center brought a new wave of terror: a sniper in the Washington suburbs. Not the mass catastrophe produced by tons of collapsing steel and burning jet fuel, the sniper's campaign wrought massive uncertainty punctuated by randomly chosen, but precisely aimed shots. Ordinary people doing ordinary things were transformed into targets, the suburbs into a shooting range. Seven fell during the first three days of the sniper's attack. "killed while sitting on a park bench," "killed while walking across a parking lot," "killed while doing lawn work," "killed while putting gas in his taxi cab," "killed while vacuuming her minivan," "killed on the street corner," "shot while loading packages into her car,"[19] each victim was a mark, frozen in a rifle's telescopic sight, isolated from his or her surroundings, a target in an exercise in marksmanship. Six more would fall before the snipers, John Allen Muhammad and John Lee Malvo, were finally apprehended. In terms of numbers, thirteen shooting deaths in the space of three weeks is hardly remarkable in the gun-crazy USA. Los Angeles alone can yield six hundred shooting deaths in a year, with the notorious South Central contributing twenty per week. Even Muhammad and Malvo's exploits might have gone unnoticed had they spread their victims out instead of concentrating them in the highly visible topography of the DC area. Indeed, prior shootings in Louisiana and Alabama that were subsequently attributed to the snipers might have remained in the homicide limbo of unsolved crime – just another random shooting death. Only by concentrating their attack, did the snipers' serial spree take on the proportion of terror to emerge as what Jean Baudrillard calls a "singularity [in] the heart of a system of generalized exchange."[20]

October was a month of relentless uncertainty, steeped in the awful reality that anyone could get a bullet through the head while pumping gas. The sniper attacks brought a lottery of death to the suburbs. The banal landscape of car-choked roadways and parking lots, the commerce of gas stations, convenience stores, and strip malls were reconfigured in a new terrain of risk. The cloak of uneventful malaise that passes for security was torn asunder to reveal a population gripped with fear and anxiety. Media and law enforcement officials issued palliatives meant to calm, all the while fanning our fears with more uncertainty. We were told that death by the sniper's bullet was a million to one shot and we were reminded that death in a car crash is far more likely than death by a random sniper. But the stakes seemed much higher since every victim was so unremarkably just like us. Beyond reason and gripped by the faith we bestow in the luck of the individual (whether good or bad), we fell prey to sniper anxiety. During the height of the sniper attacks, *USA Today* reported that Americans were more worried by the sniper than they were by impending war with Iraq and the plummeting economy. Even people far from the sniper's epicenter in places like Montana worried that the sniper would generate copy-cat versions in their own neighborhoods.[21] We, the society of rampant individualism and the culture of commodity replication (whose apparent contradiction has recently found resolution in the reported birth of the first cloned human) are doomed to the fear that every individual event will spawn its unwanted copy-cat replicant. So, we plotted the snipers' strikes on a mental map of criss-crossing interstates from Montgomery County MD to Ashland VA, wondering if the sniper would move further south or do something truly spectacular like take a plane to the West Coast and begin anew with a fresh set of victims. Our fear enhanced the aura of the sniper. The FBI provided us with a profile of an angry white man to which we added an apocryphal white van seen leaving the crime scenes. And with each day, we awaited the report of yet another unlikely – but no less chosen – individual.

The snipers' lottery of death was not an antithesis, but rather a grim counterpoint to all the ways free-market capitalism has made our lives a gamble. Rocked by accounting scandals, Enron, WorldCom, and Tyco have collapsed and with them the futures of many middle-class Americans. Like a bad hand in poker, our 401 k plans have folded. Sky rocketing medical expenses have turned seniors into crap shooters who stake their lives on whether or not a particular drug or procedure is "covered." And the policy of "school choice" has turned education into a lottery of Babel with the middle class opting to play the game of vouchers, charter, and home schools. Of the fifty states that comprise the union, most are struggling with budget shortfalls, with California and New York in the hole by billions of dollars. No wonder forty-six states have created lotteries to patch their budgets. For a population whose claim on jobs and social services is tenuous, states offer scratch and win tickets for instant cash rewards and lucky lotto numbers for big jackpots. Of course the odds of winning the lottery are equal to the odds of being shot by a sniper. But who cares, with the Constitutional guarantees of life, liberty and the pursuit of happiness nowhere in sight, we gamble to make our daily lives work. Random but fatal, the sniper's bullet is our proof that the system really is based on the luck of the draw.

The snipers' campaign of terror was waged against the suburb and cast its atomization in stark relief. Witness Karl Marx's description of a surprisingly similar landscape:

A small holding, a peasant and his family; alongside them another small holding, another peasant and another family. A few score of these make up a village, and a score of villages make up a Department. In this way, the great mass of the French nation is formed by simple addition of homologous magnitudes, much as potatoes in a sack.[22]

Would Marx have seen Montgomery Co. any differently? The sprawl of roadways, strip malls, office complexes, and condominiums engulf a landscape of homogeneous continuity. More exurb than suburb, Montgomery, Frederick, and Prince George's Counties – all prey to the snipers' attacks – are home to "a tribe of people who don't live in cities, or commute to cities, or have any contact with urban life."[23] Having fled more congested inner suburbs, exurbanites congregate in anomalous cul-de-sac neighborhoods newly gouged out of farm land and open nature. Once installed, exurbanites lobby for more highways (to facilitate their consumerist lifestyle) and less growth (to preserve their dream of escape). Wealthier than the potatoes in the sack, exurbanites are distinguished by their cell phones and other electronic devices. These embody the exurbanite's insertion in the information industry just as the potatoes figure the fruits of the peasant's labor.

Marx goes on to assess the French peasantry as a class in terms that might well be applied to exurbanites.

In so far as millions of families live under economic conditions of existence that separate their mode of life, their interests and their culture from those of other classes, and put them in hostile opposition to the latter, they form a class. In so far as there is merely a local interconnection among these small-holding peasants, and the identity of their interests begets no community, no national bond and no political organization among them, they do not form a class.[24]

The snipers' foray into the exurbs revealed a web of highways and discontinuous parking lots, an architecture of "local inter-connection" incapable of producing community. The twenty-four-hour news coverage was merciless in its quest to portray a multitude of besieged individuals, who, one-by-one, professed their unwillingness to pump gas, shop, or eat out. Their anguish bespoke a world where everything that was once familiar had suddenly become unfamiliar and threatening. Catapulted out of the mundane, they found themselves in an existential nightmare very like Jean-Paul Sartre's account of what it feels like to be apprehended by the "look" of another. Who can read *Being and Nothingness* and not remember the spine-tingling threat posed by the little house – mundane in every way, but whose windows connote the eyes of the horrible objectifying gaze? Who doesn't remember the gut-sinking humiliation of the man caught spying through a keyhole? These scenarios drawn from Sartre's experience of Nazi France capture the exurbanite's fear of scrutiny. The sniper, apt to be lurking anywhere, freezing anyone and everyone in the objectifying gaze of his telescopic sight, renders the truth of a population that always sees itself as the object of an other's judgmental look. Where the sniper's "look" produced fear and curtailment of activities, the neighbor's "look" manifests itself in the exurbanite's penchant for too-tidy houses and vacuumed minivans.

The snipers' incursions struck at the atomized and decentered reality of the exurbs where class is an ambiguous category. To the extent that exurbanites separate themselves from imperfect others – the infirm, the homeless, the poor, the unschooled, the foreign – they experience themselves as a group. But as workers, scattered across the information and service sectors, and as consumers, fetishized by their commodified desires, they produce an identity of style interests rather than class interests. They are an "us" that recognizes itself as such only when apprehended by a third party – here the sniper's gaze. Sequestered in their cul-de-sac havens, each member of the exurbanite us "feels himself trapped among an infinity of strange existences; he is alienated radically and without recourse."[25] So too in death each of the snipers' victims is immortalized as a name and a photo in the *New York Times* – the alienated indices of personhood.

Mobility is the exurbanite's excuse for freedom. The sniper curtailed this. Multi-car families, forever en route to schools and malls, found themselves immobilized and having to seek refuge in their homes. Schools became jails, "locked down" for the protection of their inmates. Privileged youth, accustomed to after-school sports, marching-band practice, homecoming festivities, and off-campus lunch breaks, were sealed in their classrooms. Apparently, the sniper as an external threat superseded memories of Colombine where the school was killing-field rather than safe haven. Besieged and imprisoned, exurbanites bemoaned their lack of freedom in newspapers whose front pages simultaneously ran stories of curfew in the West Bank. Americans and Palestinians "locked down," each the obverse of the other's reality. Thus, the sniper rendered to the American middle class an experience roughly analogous (although not in degree) to the experience produced by that class's support of US foreign policy. Habitually disconnected from the global effects of its politics, the American middle class can only know itself by indirection.

In writing *The Eighteenth Brumaire*, Marx strove to document the waning of Revolutionary France and its transformation into a bureaucratic state. Part and parcel was the figure of Louis Bonaparte whose base of support was the small-holding peasants, who, because they did not truly form a class, could not "represent themselves" but "must be represented."[26] George Bush, the younger, is our Louis Bonaparte. And just as the latter represented history as farce, the second coming of a Napoleon, so too, is our current Bush a farcical second coming of the first Bush presidency complete with a second Gulf War.

Extending the logic of repetition as farce into the virtual, Jean Baudrillard has argued that Desert Storm, the first Gulf War, is the war that never happened (*La Guerre du Golfe n'a pas eu lieu*). Although, as the most televised war, he concedes that it "devoured space and time." And it devoured us as well. Glued to our televisions, we watched CNN's Peter Arnette, hunkered down in Baghdad while incoming missiles flared behind him. Did we pause to consider that all the other images that filled our twenty-four-hour news addiction were a video feed direct from the Pentagon? We needed Arnette's reality to lend credence to the whole show. Enthralled, we sat at our TV monitors and watched a war portrayed as a video game. Positioned to appreciate all the new technologies deployed for Desert Storm, we got high. A viewing public absorbed into a war rendered virtual, we achieved the "consensus of a flat line encephalograph."[27]

If the Gulf War was portrayed as an easy victory for the Americans, it wasn't an easy defeat for Iraq, where 1.3 million died as a direct result of either the war or the post-war sanctions.[28] But the war has had its second coming for us. Indeed, America may have to reconsider its sweeping victory in the light of the Gulf War's boomerang effect. According to Congressional testimony, "Since the Gulf War ended in 1991, there has been a growing number of reports of chronic illness among the nearly 700,000 US troops who served in Saudi Arabia, Kuwait, and Iraq."[29] Preparing to fight a dirty war, fueled by fears that the Iraqis would use chemical and biological weapons, the US military inoculated its soldiers with experimental drug cocktails. And to blast Iraqi tanks sky high, the Pentagon issued depleted-uranium ordinance. The result is a veteran population whose chronic symptoms include "memory loss, fatigue, sore muscles and joints, insomnia, cough, some night sweats, diverticulitis, diarrhea, kidney stones, bloody stools, growth on [the] eye, rashes, tingling and itching sensations, and depression and irritability."[30] Contrary to the weight of veteran testimony before the Congress, the official government position is that Gulf War Syndrome does not exist.

Just as the Gulf War comes back to haunt us as a malady, so too, our sniper, John Allen Muhammad, is our angel of death returned from the battlefield to visit the fruits of his marksmanship upon the civilian population. Actually, Muhammad was not a combatant in Desert Storm, but an engineer, something of a glorified laborer. Not content with tearing down Iraqi fortifications and building roads, Muhammad practiced marksmanship and routinely won awards for his skill.

Though the United States is forever eager to find military solutions to dilemmas that are at heart political and economic, there has been some post-9/11 discussion that broaches the question of why the US was the target of such blatant hostility. Of course, George Bush tells us time and again that the terrorists hate our freedoms – this, while his administration is busy assigning our freedoms to Homeland Security and the Office of Information Awareness. Not to fear, with scoundrels like John Poindexter and Henry Kissinger – both newly resurrected and laundered – freedom will surely prevail. Nevertheless, a few contrary journalists have been so bold as to raise the question of US imperialism as a factor in the terrorist attacks. Even the word "Empire" has come up, although it doesn't appear that any of the talking heads has read Hardt and Negri. When Empire is mentioned it tends to elide with imperialism to produce a map of America's military outposts in places like Djibouti, Kazakhstan, Qatar and Afghanistan.

Imperialism is perceived as necessary, even beneficial to the world's health – notwithstanding all those broken treaties occasioned by US unilateralism.

If the discussion of imperialism should veer slightly to the left so as to allow a few NPR liberals to be heard, blame becomes self-criticism. Fingers point with embarrassment at all those nasty thugs – like bin Laden – who we supported in our previous military incarnation as the world's Cold Warrior. Liberal commentators have coined terms like "blowback" and "boomerang" to explain why we were targeted. Essentially, we reaped the rewards of our bad investments.

What's interesting about "blowback" and "boomerang" is the way these terms work to preserve cause-and-effect reasoning. America projects its policies into the world, these provoke certain responses which, then, boomerang back to us. It conjures a "tit for tat" world demarcated by a sense of here (the homeland) and there (the foreign). Such thinking fails to apprehend how US imperialism, now, at the advent of the twenty-first century, enacts empire as a continuous globalized circuit of control and domination. There is no "here" and "there," but rather a Moebius strip on a global scale. Ubiquitous in Lacanian thought, the Moebius strip "describes the subject, where the apparent division of conscious and repressed turns out to be [a] unity of writing on one continuous side."[31] Similarly, the world defined by global capitalism flattens difference in the drive to produce a continuous circuit of production and exchange. Under the logic of Moebius, everything we perceive as a duality – inside/outside, sign/referent, self/other – everything capable of generating contradiction, is sublimely subsumed as a continuous circularity. In an essay that has also circled the globe, Jean Baudrillard bates self-righteous America and maintains, in Moebius fashion, that the 9/11 terrorists were not our absolute "other," but objects of our own creation. As he puts it, "the increase in the power of power heightens the will to destroy it. And it was party to its own destruction."[32] So too, our sniper is not "other" but us, our Gulf War enacted on the homefront, here to exact the collateral damage that our war daily wreaks on Iraqis, here to give a lie to the notion of a zero-death war, our safe technological alibi. Here/there, us/them, we all become ciphers on a global map of war become universally domestic, universally acceptable.

The lead up to our second war with Iraq generated a daily litany of the threats we face: dirty bombs in our cities, anthrax in our mail, dockside containers loaded with chemical agents, bombs that explode power plants into nuclear chain reactions, dams primed to inundate whole states – images of mass destruction so ever-present they lost their sting. Accomplices, we invented video games that feature simulated weapons of mass destruction. These we played while we watched CNN's persistent warnings of Iraq's WMDs. Only the sniper was able to blast through the banality of ever-present threat. A bolt of fantasmic reality, he struck without warning, leaving only bullet casings and an occasional ransom note as proof of his existence and testament his victims did not die a natural death.

"No man is ever an individual, it would be better to call him a universal singular."[33] This is how Sartre considers the relationship between individual freedom and historical necessity. "Totalized and thereby universalized by his epoch, he retotalizes his epoch in the course of reproducing himself in his epoch as a singularity."[34] The sniper, an isolated and aberrant freedom, a singularity that evaded FBI attempts to profile him, is simultaneously our truth and the truth of our epoch. Soldier/civilian, black man/father to a surrogate son (the son an immigrant, one of the "Huddled masses yearning to breathe free"), the sniper embodies our society's dearly held family values. Who can forget the front-page photo of Muhammad and Malvo, shown seated on a couch in a homey ambiance, the two of them grinning from ear to ear. The photo presented the pair as poster child and father for the sort of male role models that the dominant society has exhorted African Americans to develop ever since the Monyhan report condemned the female-headed, single-parent family as root cause of black poverty and crime. How remarkable that every front page across America greeted its readers with the ineffable discontinuity between the photo that conjured a healthy, happy father/son relationship and the headline that proclaimed the two as cold-hearted snipers. All our society's dearly held ideals of fathering are in Muhammad upheld and twisted to reveal a dark antithesis: Muhammad, the caregiver who sheltered a fatherless immigrant; Muhammad the nurturer who taught his son the value of good nutrition and exercise; Muhammad, the mentor who taught his disciple the manly art of marksmanship; Muhammad, the coach who recognized his son's talents could be put to advantageous use in the trunk of their car; Muhammad, the altruistic who allowed his protégé to share in the killing. Thus, with a twist like the Moebius strip, Muhammad reveals his fatherly universality as a murderous singularity, which is in no way aberrant because death-dealing force is our nation's most fundamental truth.

Ours is a world dramatically strayed from the path envisioned more than a century ago by Hegel, for whom history moved inexorably towards the realization of Reason. Ours, the reason of global capitalism, moves towards the perfection of superpower domination. Where Hegel saw certain "great individuals" capable of grasping history's trajectory "to make it their own end,"[35] we produce an antithetical non-hero whose violent acts render visible our history's course. Where Hegel saw world-historical individuals like Napoleon as vehicles for the realization of history, our history produces a sniper. Neither our world's negation, nor our contradiction, the sniper manifests the "cunning of reason"[36] no longer synonymous with the workings of Spirit, but rather the banality of global capital.

As vehicle of history, the sniper mimics and reveals to us the reality of our latest war technology. Out of the blue, his death bullets capture the essence of our new war toy, the Predator. An unmanned surveillance plane armed with Hellfire anti-tank missiles, the Predator strikes targeted individuals without warning. And it kills while preserving zero-death security for its "pilot" who guides the craft from a ground installation hundreds of miles away. Thus the United States launched its sniper attack on Qaed Salim Sinan al-Harethi, killed by the Predator while driving in a car with five other individuals in Yemen. No more remote than the streets and parking lots of the DC suburbs, the hinterland is under surveillance. Anyone anywhere can be targeted by a console jockey logging missions from inside a bunker.

The quintessential embodiment of our moment in history, the sniper manifests the repercussions of US imperialism on the homefront. With military surveillance planes patrolling the skies over Washington and ground troops including 623 agents from the Bureau of Alcohol, Tobacco, and Firearms, 600 FBI agents, 100 US Marshals, and 50 Secret Service agents,[37] the quest for the sniper transformed a police action into a Federal mobilization. Americans, lulled by the myth of democracy, like to imagine that imperialism is something we enact elsewhere. We fail to grasp the ever-present military in our daily lives. Yet many of us live in cities that border military camps like Tacoma WA, a place the sniper once called home. Here, FBI agents dug a tree stump out of his backyard and hauled it back to Washington where they pried out the bullets that would match the spent casings found at murder sites thousands of miles away. Military cities like Tacoma precariously survive a pathological symbiosis between town (a site for off-duty R and R and the domestic life of military dependents) and base (our nation's most viable welfare economy). Journeying to Tacoma to get a feel for the sniper's neighborhood, a reporter for the *New York Times* commented, "You can't drive around Tacoma without noticing the transitory nature of an Army town, with neighborhoods that are used and reused, where people move on without anyone noticing."[38] Here, the sniper's backyard target practice also went unnoticed, camouflaged by the bigger booms of the heavy artillery guns at Fort Lewis. Less substantial than the potatoes in a sack – the small-holding exurbanites who claim their political presence with their conservative votes – the transient population falls through the cracks, fails to register, until one of them travels to the sprawling megalopolis and begins picking off citizens.

The sniper straddles the blurred boundary between military and civilian life that is fast becoming every American's common lot. His car, a 1990 Chevy Caprice that he bought for $250, was camouflaged as unremarkable. Indeed, the police stopped him ten times during the course of his exploits and each time let him pass through their roadblocks because neither he nor his car appeared on any pertinent database. As a *Washington Post* writer put it, the sniper was "Hiding in plain sight."[39] He slept at a YMCA or in his car, ate a brownie at a sandwich shop, and ordered pizza from a room at an Econo Lodge. Not unlike the 9/11 terrorists who blended into the suburban mainstream, the sniper was an everyman. Musing over the banality of American everyday life that offered "cover and camouflage"[40] to the 9/11 terrorists, Baudrillard points to a complicity that enabled the terrorists to hide in plain sight. He asks, "Might not any inoffensive person be a potential terrorist? If they could pass unnoticed, then each of us is a criminal going unnoticed (every plane becomes suspect),"[41] indeed every nondescript car. Contrary to its mundane appearance, the sniper's car was a hybrid vehicle that straddled civilian and military spheres. The trunk made over into a shooting space with sight holes bored through the steel, the Caprice was a light-infantry assault vehicle. Finally, the sniper's weapon, a Bushmaster XM-15, also straddles military and civilian designations. According to the manufacturer, the Bushmaster is "a civilian version of the standard American military rifle, the M-16,"[42] a perfect choice for a military-trained marksman operating on civilian soil.

His rifle, a civilian copy of a military weapon; his car, a light infantry vehicle; himself, an erstwhile soldier living in an Army town; his modus operandi, a military protocol, the sniper delineates the military takeover of everyday life and the spread of the battlefield to the homefront. Significantly the category of soldier has been further sliced and hybridized to create the notion of "illegal combatants." Where the Taliban has been consigned to the limbo of Guantanamo, which is administered by the US Army but not subject to the laws of either the United States or Cuba, Muhammad and Malvo as boomerang soldiers have been assigned to Federal Court.

As the global Moebius strip erodes distinctions between battlefield/homefront, soldier/civilian, who, then, is the enemy? According to Catherine Lutz, anthropologist of the homefront, civilians are increasingly at risk and can find themselves in the position of enemy. The end of the draft has professionalized the Army. No longer every man's common lot, soldiering is a choice as is civilian life. And civilians are of necessity defined as weak, dependent on the Army for their protection. Yet many civilians have better lives than their counterparts in the Army, hence the makings of a new sort of class antagonism between those who preserve and protect and those who bring home fat pay checks.

Recently, in the Army town/base, Fayetteville/Fort Bragg, four soldiers, three of them special ops, returned from duty in Afghanistan and killed their wives. Once shock gave way to attempts at explanation, journalists and military experts offered an array of rationales from the chemical (the side effects of an anti-malaria drug) to the psychological (everything from post-traumatic stress syndrome to the specific difficulties faced by military families). Similarly, the media has sought to explain the sniper – the child of a broken home, lack of a father figure, a control freak with a short temper, inability to form long-term relationships. What's not mentioned is that all the victims are civilians – people lifted out of their ordinary lives and put in the place of the enemy. Did anyone question why the snipers, both of them black, showed no sense of racial preference in their choice of targets? Black/white, young/old, male/female – all our census categories were filled with victims, thus denying us the possibility of calling these "hate crimes." The only common characteristic of the dead is their civilian status. Mobilized for a suburban military action, the snipers targeted civilians, not as collateral damage (people inadvertently killed for their proximity to a designated enemy), but targets chosen for want of a more clearly defined enemy – or perhaps chosen because the civilian has become the enemy.

The final days of the snipers' campaign overlapped with another story on the global Moebius strip: Chechen rebels had stormed a Moscow theater and were holding hundreds of audience and cast members hostage. The siege dragged on for days, usually appearing on page three of the *New York Times* with accounts of the sniper on page one. What bumped Moscow's story to the front page was its final solution to the hostage crisis. Deftly and ruthlessly the Russians pumped an as yet undisclosed poison gas into the theater, mortally asphyxiating rebels and hostages alike. Emblazoned across newspapers everywhere, our snipers' discreet war against civilians found itself juxtaposed with the Russians' dirty war against civilians.

If there is a final truth that the sniper conveys, it is our readiness to wage war on civilians.

4

ONLY THE SHADOW KNOWS

During the months following 9/11, at the same time that the US Postal Service had to contend with the anthrax-laced letters, it also had to decide what to do with "heaps of mail addressed to Osama bin Laden."[43] Most of these letters were sent on to Afghanistan before investigators from the Justice Department could obtain a warrant authorizing a search of the letters. As none of the letters was ever opened (except perhaps by Osama), we can only speculate as to their content. Certainly many would have conveyed threats. Americans suffering the trauma of attack and wanting to take immediate action could well have poured all their anger and frustration into a letter addressed to the perpetrator of their rage. Can there be sufficient invective in the English language to express such anger? Maybe some of the letters were laced with anthrax.

It's more likely, though, that the letters were infused with perfume. Isn't it conceivable that many of the women who reported to their analysts that they were haunted by the dream of sleeping with bin Laden took the opportunity to pen the terrorist a letter of seduction? Would the ghastly, aesthetic face of Osama flash a smile upon opening a love letter from an American? Or would such a letter be the kiss of death, a defilement more toxic than anthrax?

Whether curse or seduction, the letters bespeak a naive attachment to the real. At a time when most Americans send electronic letters, e-mails to colleagues, family members, friends, businesses, and institutions, a page (handwritten or typed) folded in an envelope, stamped, addressed, and designated for actual physical transport represents a tangible link to a longed for real. Letters sent to Osama enact a form of sympathetic magic whereby the phantom terrorist, that haunting visage seen on video feeds from Al-Jazeera, becomes a man of flesh, blood, and bone. In the same way that thousands of American children write letters to Santa Claus at the North Pole, we wrote letters to Osama in Afghanistan. The child's letter is meant to dispel disbelief. It confirms Santa as real by the logic that equates a real letter with a real recipient. Similarly, Osama, inscrutably mythic to the western imagination, and Afghanistan, remote as the North Pole, are pressed into the mold of the real by the fact of the letters.

This, the age of fundamentalisms – both Christian and Islamic – is an era of obtuse literal mindedness anchored in a devotion to the real. Where the nineteenth century gave birth to the forensic sciences, popularized by the ploy of the fingerprint in detective novels, we now boast a host of technologies guaranteed to inscribe us in the real: voice prints, retinal scans, and DNA. And where Marshall McLuhan once shocked the world by proclaiming the "medium is the message," thus indicating that meaning was no longer rooted in what was said but in how it was communicated, we have now entered a world where the code is reality. The human genome is our meaning. Struggling to keep up with advances in science, the government's newly created Office of Homeland Security seems antiquated at its inception. Attempting to pave the way to the real, it compiles information on us – our credit card purchases, our travel, our e-mail, our medical records. Missing the mark of the real, Homeland Security constructs us as the imaginary sum of our data. With the imaginary steeped in the tedium of information, and the real reduced to the barren skeleton of the code, we risk becoming a nation of sleepwalkers, yearning to recover the remnant of the symbolic order in our dreams.

While a reductive reading of Lacan preaches the symbolic, the imaginary, and the real as discrete categories, the letters to Osama manifest a blurring of the boundaries whereby the symbolic impinges on the imaginary so as to force the real into being. The result is a version of the real that only exists as a fiction. In a series of essays on the post-9/11 state of the real,

Slavoj Žižek recommends that "we should be able to discern, in what we experience as fiction, the hard kernel of the Real which we are able to sustain only if we fictionalize it."[44] Surely, the investigators from the Justice Department would have been able to discern the "hard kernel of the Real" if they had been allowed access to the letters. Undoubtedly, such a kernel would have provided a basis for bringing the letter writers to trial – or, in a turn to the irreal, consigning them to the limbo of illegal aiders and abettors of terror. Sadly, such kernels would reduce the real to banality. Far more interesting are the kernels that will never be known to us, these imbricated in each letter writer's private fiction.

What haunts the post-9/11 world is the specter of the real, the horror that we might one day exceed the code yellow and orange alerts and go all the way to red. Only then will we know what a real catastrophe is. Not these sporadic and isolated events – a Trade Tower here an anthrax letter there – but the final big bang that will not only validate Bush, Cheney, and Rumsfeld, but obliterate them with it. The ultimate bang is as much a figment of the imagination as the notion of an ultimate real somehow "concealed beneath the layers of imaginary and symbolic veils."[45] Calling this "the ultimate appearance,"[46] Žižek argues that the notion of an ultimate and absolutely distilled "Real Thing is a fantasmatic spectre whose presence guarantees the consistency of our symbolic edifice."[47]

Nowhere is the fantasmatic quality of the real more apparent than in our own shadow government. How stunned – and bemused – we were to discover some six months after the attack on the WTC that not only do we have a shadow government, but its "secure, undisclosed location"[48] is exactly where Vice President Dick Cheney hid out during the aftermath of 9/11. The shadow government is based in forty underground bunkers built into the mountains within a 100-mile radius of Washington, our own Tora Bora. Some of these sites are no longer "undisclosed." For instance, there is Mount Weather in Virginia, designated hideout for the Speaker of the House, Cabinet Heads, and the Supreme Court Justices. No mean Afghan cave, Mount Weather would be Nirvana for the Taliban. Described as a "small city,"[49] it includes "vast quantities of office space, room to store the nation's art treasures, [and] sleeping accommodations for several thousand people."[50] That it can double as shelter and tomb is evident in two other features: "a private reservoir and a crematorium."[51] Maybe our government is planning for its own martyrdom.

Besides Mount Weather, there is Raven Rock, the underground site for whatever remnant of the military manages to survive a nuclear attack on Washington. This site includes "computers and communication gear ... a barbershop [for those military cuts], dental and medical clinics, and a chapel"[52] (in case anyone wants to appeal to a higher authority). Leaked descriptions of the furnishings and decor of all sites characterize them as '50s efficiency. Indeed, many of the bunkers were first built under Eisenhower and replicate on a grand scale the fallout shelters that many Americans dug in their back yards.

In reinventing the bunkers, our postmodern state betrays its nostalgia for the simple "us versus them" politics of the Cold War. Oh, for a clearly discernable enemy; hence the utility of Saddam Hussein who enabled us to evade the messy uncertainty posed by a diffuse network of terrorists. What could be more concrete than a bunker carved into the heart of a mountain? – Proof of an enemy real as rock.

As the bunkers' referential point of origin, the '50s represent the fantasized ur-moment of our history, a time before the social upheavals wrought by the movements for Civil Rights and women's equality, not to mention the war in Vietnam. This is the time when we imagine the nuclear family really did exist, a mirage that we turned into a fact a decade later in the TV sit-com, *Leave It To Beaver*. The show gave us the image of the '50s family as a memorable reality which we have continued to inscribe in our popular culture imaginary for subsequent renditions of the same Mom and Pop scenario. Just visit the Prime Time Diner at Disney World and you will find "Mom" in her apron serving up a healthy dinner of meatloaf, mashed potatoes, and Jell-O for dessert. With every enactment, culture stages the '50s as our socially centered reality. Happy, then, the employees of the shadow government who are dispatched back in time to their bunkers. As actors in a top-secret drama, they're only allowed to tell their families that they're off "on a business trip."[53]

Here, we strike the kernel of reality in the midst of subterfuge. It is the privilege of the patriarchal breadwinner whose comings and goings the '50s housewife knew not to question. This, catapulted into the twenty-first century and recreated in the post apocalyptic shadow government. Underground twenty-four hours a day and on ninety-day rotations, these breadwinners entombed in a bureaucratic purgatory must dream of the freedom of their '50s counterpart: the traveling salesman whose "business trip" would have included the pastimes of a cheap hotel whose efficiency decor would be proper setting for the pleasures of whisky and a compliant woman. What do the hundreds of employees relegated to the shadow government do all day – and night? Presumably nothing, as the real government has yet to be hit. None of the accounts of their caves mention video libraries stockpiled with morale boosters like Bruce Willis' *Die Hard*, *1* and *2* or, more to the point, *Armageddon*, where Willis saves the earth from a catastrophic collision with an asteroid. Maybe, though, in keeping with the '50s as referential point of origin, members of the shadow government are only allowed to bring photos and videos of their families. Not unlike California school children who are urged to pack a family photo in their earthquake kits along with the essentials (a flashlight, bottled water, and nutritious snacks), shadow government employees are probably forced to live the ideology of a panic intended to preserve the family as the core of American life. Bruce Willis will not be allowed in a real catastrophe, not even in his imaginary incarnations. Then, too, family photos might also be prohibited in the bunkers. How else to maintain secrecy? Unlike those messy Al Qaeda operatives caught with their telltale paraphernalia: journals, letters, photos, videos, cell phones, and laptops, America's shadow government should vanish into its bunkers without a trace. As shadows of the real, they must be utterly anonymous.

Thus we come full circle from the rock-hard concrete to the insubstantial, from the bunker government configured as the real referent for the symbolic performance of George Bush, to the existing government rendered real on the basis of a shadowy, non-functioning void. Similarly, Žižek documents "the fundamental paradox of our 'passion for the Real': it culminates in its apparent opposite, in a theatrical spectacle."[54] On the eve of Bush's inauguration, many Americans saw Dick Cheney as the power behind the throne, the heavyweight, the reality principle to Bush the inept, befuddled figurehead of state. Such an interpretation was confirmed by Bush himself when (in his usual presidential prose) he explained that he felt "an obligation as president [to] put measures in place that, should somebody be successful in attacking Washington DC [would guarantee] there's an ongoing government ... That's one reason why the vice president was going to undisclosed locations."[55] In this scenario, the President is expendable, a visible target; while the Vice President is preserved as the actually existing source of continuity. But if Cheney spends most of his heir-apparent life underground, aren't we apt to forget him? True, he does surface from time to time to attend equally shadowy meetings with energy executives after which all documents are either shredded or sequestered. Thus, the heavyweight becomes phantom and the lightweight becomes real.

Lecturing on the famous play within a play in *Hamlet*, wherein Hamlet vows to catch the "conscience of the king," Jacques Lacan proposes that the play scene registers truth in fiction. Hamlet uses the play to create a structure, a dimension of "truth disguised"[56] as a fiction in order to make Claudius betray himself. Here, the real is not a kernel, conveniently rock hard and discernable in our fictions, but is instead the very structure of our fictions. So it's not what the play narrates (Claudius pouring the poison in the erstwhile king's ear), but the play scene as a structure that reveals the truth of Hamlet's Oedipal quandary. In seeing the play scene, Hamlet apprehends himself allied with his father's murderer and complicit with him in the desire for his mother.

America's play within a play reveals a different structure. Not the incest of Oedipus, but the incest of cloned replicants. Indeed, the elaborate underground system of bunkers is not our only shadow government. Weekly on NBC, the Bush White House is shadowed by the fictional presidency of Josiah Bartlett of TV's *The West Wing*. Inaugurated during the Clinton era, Martin Sheen's rendition of the President was a left-liberal dream come true. While Clinton was busy instituting a neo-conservative economic agenda and driving coffin nails into welfare and health care, Jed Bartlett was fighting to maintain our social safety net. Because *The West Wing* was so clearly Clinton's foil, many devoted viewers felt the show would lose its relevance with the Bush presidency. The fictional Bartlett and the real Bush would simply be polar opposites, unable to generate grist for utopian desires.

While *The West Wing* narratives are indeed liberal fantasies, the real key to understanding the role the show plays may be found in yet another fictional shadow government. Unveiled on CBS's *60 Minutes*, a revival of *Point, Counterpoint* pits Bill Clinton against Bob Dole who square off and sound off on a weekly basis. In their debates, the former President and the former presidential candidate shadow the Bush government with alternative visions of what once was and what once might have been. Thus, viewers can experience a full range of parallel realities (Bartlett intervened and saved the day in a Rwanda-like genocide), all the while de-realizing the Bush narrative. Here, the question is not which presidency is a fiction and which is the real, or whether the unseen Vice President is the true puppet master. Rather, the structure of all these clones tells the truth of the Bush presidency, itself a fiction produced out of voter fraud and Supreme Court chicanery. Not that Al Gore then emerges as the last bastion of the real. Neither shadow nor real, Gore has become taboo, the homo sacer of the political world. Notwithstanding his desperate attempts to make himself real by putting on weight, growing a beard, and speaking out against the President's war policy, Gore lost his chance to be a shadow when he was summarily cancelled as a political personage in Florida. Only true replicants and shadows can play at being President because the truth of the presidency is its clones whose function is to diffuse reality across a spectrum of fictions.

The structure of cloning lends its truth to more than the presidency. Indeed we all had the opportunity to structure our daily lives as a clone of the shadow government when Tom Ridge, head of Homeland Security, suggested we turn a room into an impromptu fallout shelter. His advice came during one of the orange alerts when Americans were admonished to be extra vigilant. To channel our anxieties into constructive shopping and home maintenance, Ridge advised that a simple application of plastic sheeting and duct tape could seal a room against chemical attack. The numbers of people who raced out to buy duct tape were equal to the numbers who concocted jokes about duct tape. In the end, Ridge retracted his advice when he realized that some Americans might prematurely hole up in their plastic cocoons and suffocate without ever getting to test their shelters in a real chemical attack.

By far the best bunker clones were the war protesters who turned up at demonstrations wrapped head to toe in plastic sheeting and duct tape. These turned their bodies into metaphors and in so doing resurrected the symbolic. Their antitheses are the war protesters who flocked to Baghdad as human shields. One strategy was to ring Baghdad with a wall of human shields. The reduced model was to place token shields in sensitive target areas. In either case, the body as shield usurps metaphor and offers itself as a real (although puny) buffer to attack.

While the attack on the WTC killed 3000 people, it failed to extinguish the high-profile investment companies lodged in the towers. This is because businesses, unlike people, clone their operations into backup files. For instance, "Fiduciary Trust lost 87 of its 647 employees in the towers. [But] despite the tragic loss of life and the disappearance of its hardware infrastructure, the company was quickly up and running from a Comdisco recovery center located in New Jersey."[57] Comdisco is one of many data management companies that offer secure storage for the materials that constitute business as a physical body. The leader in supplying bunkers to business is Iron Mountain which operates six hundred facilities worldwide, eight of them hundreds of feet underground. Like the bunkers for our shadow government, Iron Mountain's facilities also originated in the Cold War. Apparently, we envisioned the need to save documents as well as people from Soviet attack. Today Iron Mountain provides storage (and shredding capabilities) "for all major media, including paper, computer disks and tapes, microfilm and microfiche, master audio and video tapes, films and optical disks, x-rays and blueprints."[58] Contrary to popular belief, the age of the computer has not made paper obsolete, but has instead generated a greater need for paper and other types of backup files.

One of Iron Mountain's recently acquired facilities is a vast limestone mine north of Pittsburgh. Formerly home to government documents, this facility once "stored applications from every person who ever sought a Social Security number."[59] Now its catacombs will become final resting place for the Bettman Archive of 75 million photo originals. At "-4 degrees Fahrenheit and 35 percent relative humidity"[60] the limestone mine guarantees life everlasting to the image of the young John Kennedy Jr. saluting his father's coffin.

The life-in-death preserved entombment of our documents betrays a stubborn attachment for the real at a time when copies drive consumption. CDs and CD-ROMs, mini disks and DVDs render VHS and audiotapes obsolete like the phonograph records of yesteryear. Rather than supplanting the need for an original, the copy craves its real and demands that we designate some copies as more real than others. Bunkered documents become the real, all the more so because we'll never see them. Instead they'll be scanned for us and transmitted to our eyeballs through our computers. Is this Walter Benjamin's dream come true of the democratized work of art? According to Benjamin, the mechanical reproduction of art has the powerful effect of eliminating the aura of traditional art – its privileged uniqueness – precisely because it delivers a copy to "the beholder or listener in his own particular situation."[61] Benjamin celebrated the copy and saw in it "the tremendous shattering of tradition"[62] that was directly opposed to fascism's treasuring of tradition. Post-fascist and post-modern, we have concretized certain lucky copies as real. Buried in mines that no longer function to meet the needs of the bygone steel industry and the subsequent bureaucracy of the '50s, these copies become the designated referents for the millions of clones that circulate above ground in and out of our homes, shops, libraries, and institutions. Essentially, we stepped into the brave new virtual world and immediately jumped back into Plato's cave where "the truth [is] literally nothing but the shadows of images."[63] The conceit of the cave recasts the notion of a play within a play, this time not from Hamlet's point of view but rather the point of view of the actor/spectators in the play. Ignorant of how the interplay of light on objects creates shadows, they "see only their shadows"[64] and concoct a sublime world where reality is the imaginary. However, Plato, obliged to disabuse them of their mystification, expands the optic to show that the shadows are mere appearance. In contrast to Plato's cave, Iron Mountain allows us to overcome the need for demystification because it enables us to make our shadows real.

And what better way to do so than with home radar as the ultimate security device. Developed as one of the miracles of World War II, radar was thoroughly mythologized in the '50s for a generation of school children confronting the contradictions of science and technology. While Disney was busy touting nuclear energy as the housewife's companion by offering cartoons of nuclear-powered vacuums and toasters, we were being drilled in how to "duck and cover" under our desks. In an atmosphere of Cold War anxiety, science teachers undoubtedly found relief in telling the tale of how we stole radar from the bat. Like Lévi-Strauss recounting a Borroro myth, the teacher explained the bat's magic of using sound waves to render objects, if not visible, then readable. Indeed, bat physics could overcome the metaphysical question of whether an object must be seen, or heard, to be real. In fact, radar can give us a shadow where we thought there was nothing.

No longer a technology reserved for the military (witness the hundreds of radar devices and their applications advertised on the Internet), radar offers unlimited possibilities for securing private spaces. Where many homes today are equipped with motion-triggered outdoor lighting systems, the suburban home of the not too distant future may well be secured with a radar device like the one currently produced by Israel Aircraft Industries. Marketed as suitable for "officials' residences"[65] the Minder, which can be installed along a fence line, is ready to be democratized to meet the bunkering needs of private families. Indeed, the Minder is only one example of hundreds of available lightweight and portable radar systems, some specifically designed to be mounted on SUVs. Once radar becomes a standard automotive accessory (like the GPS navigating system), suburbanites will be able to stow their shovels and duct tape for the convenience of a family-sized mobile bunker. That is until someone, like the war protester clothed in plastic sheeting and duct tape, applies anti-radar stealth paint to his body and becomes an anti-matter real threat that the Minder can't translate into a shadow.

Actually shadow invasions happen on a regular basis in North Carolina where the Army conducts Operation Robin Sage four times a year. Intended to give Green Beret trainees a taste of unconventional warfare, Robin Sage is a play within a play whose consequences can be deadly. According to the military's scenario, ten of the state's central counties – all rural and somewhat impoverished – are scripted as the beleaguered nation of Pineland which has been taken over by a repressive government. The play begins when "some 200 aspiring Green

Berets [are] inserted behind 'enemy lines' by parachute, helicopter or plane."[66] Their mission is to topple Pineland's puppet government.

The distinction between fiction and reality is considerably blurred because civilian locals are recruited to play various parts. Sometimes they represent members of the resistance, but they can just as easily be guerrilla fighters allied with the tyrannical government. Costumes offer no help in discerning who's military and who's civilian. Actors from the real Army might wear camouflage but because the script calls for unconventional war, they can also don civilian attire. Similarly the locals, carried away with enthusiasm for their parts, often purchase their own camouflage clothing from the state's numerous Army Surplus Stores. Residents have been known to "construct fake bombs from PVC and traffic cones"[67] and a few "have also bought their own semiautomatic rifles for use in the exercises."[68]

Staged over a period of weeks, its scenes and acts occurring randomly across a "4,500 square mile swath"[69] of countryside, the play is sporadic and unpredictable. What lends excitement are the weapons. According to the Army's script, no real soldier may carry live ammunition. But because North Carolina is a gun-toting state, citizens would be foolish not to duck and cover at the sound of gunfire. Thus, when Jessica Keeling "heard a spray of mock machine gun fire behind the Citgo filling station … she quickly locked the doors, herded customers playing video poker into the store's walk-in refrigerator and dialed 911."[70] Jessica Keeling was an unscripted local, who without knowing it fulfilled a role in what turned out to be a hostage rescue scene staged by the Army at the auto body shop next door. Other unscripted locals have been chased and rounded up by military operatives who mistake them for locals scripted as guerrilla fighters. And one unscripted elderly couple was recently held at gunpoint in their home by soldiers decked out in face paint, camouflage, and M-4 carbines.

In a dramatization that took place in 2002, one incident stands out as a show-stopper. It involved three categories of players: two scripted soldiers disguised as locals and, hence, wearing civilian clothes; a scripted local designated as the soldiers' driver who furnished his own civilian vehicle for use in the scene, and an unscripted local Sheriff's Deputy. The scene began when the Deputy ordered the vehicle to pull over. Presuming the Deputy to be a guerrilla fighter who had stolen the uniform of a law enforcement official, the soldiers went for their duffle bag where they had what the Deputy recognized as a disassembled rifle. Responding instantly to the perceived threat, the Deputy shot the two men, one of them fatally. As an unscripted local in a real law enforcement role, the Deputy carried live ammunition. In reality, the Deputy didn't know he was in a play, and the soldiers could only surmise that the Deputy was an actor.

More complicated than Hamlet's mousetrap, Operation Robin Sage is a play within a play that defines its larger world as equally a fiction. If the various renditions of the shadow government reveal that the truth is a clone, Robin Sage demonstrates that only death is real. The Deputy's fatal act opens a Pandora's box of possible meanings. One of these casts the Deputy as a neo-conservative Hamlet who lashes out at life's blurred edges by driving the hard wedge of reality between truth and fiction. Another version sees the Deputy as a beleaguered civil servant who kills a representative of a larger, stronger Federal force in a desperate attempt to reclaim jurisdictional rights to the Homeland. In this reading the Army (not the fictional government of Pineland) is the invader. Both interpretations contain kernels of truth but neither explains the sort of world that exists around our nation's military bases. Here, there is no clear distinction between military and civilian life. Locals are either former soldiers, spouses of soldiers, or employees in businesses that cater to soldiers. They are the shadows whose real lives feed the needs of the military, who in turn see themselves defending the lives of the locals.

Commenting on the new world order and its new forms of warfare, Žižek asks "are not 'international terrorists organizations' the obscene double of the big multinational corporations – the ultimate rhizomatic machine ...?"[71] While terrorists and corporations tell different narratives, they are united by a common deterritorialized global structure. As such, they demonstrate that contradictions at the level of narrative are overcome by a rhizomatic truth that spans the globe to sprout here and there in the guise of locally specific entities.

The counties surrounding the Army's Fort Bragg in North Carolina may appear nondescript, a tangle of pine forest, farms, fields, and forsaken townships. But the appearance of abandonment belies a compaction of global capitalism's rhizomatic structure. Not a far-flung network binding terrorist to multinational corporation, but a microcosmic spot on the map where points of difference are fused to produce hybrid entities. Here, the rhizomatic structure forms a dense, entangled mass which gives rise to myriad permutations of manipulated soldier and civilian DNA. Here, the shadow other is subsumed in the self, and the bunker is the world all around.

5

THE GREATEST SHOW ON EARTH

Three Years after the attack on the World Trade Center, our nation's immediate experience of "shock and awe" has given way to a deep miasmic sense of uncertainty and dread. Doubt comes from all directions and is not limited to abiding fears that terrorists might strike again. It is largely fueled by the media where sensationalism, mixed messages, and a considerable number of downright lies are rampant.

Daily economic reports have us wallowing in the benefits of tax cuts and consuming ourselves out of recession. The stock market is on an upturn, and Wall Street seems to have survived revelations that a great number of CEOs are practiced in the art of scamming. But our nation's debt is sky high, the dollar is weak, and most jobs worth having are flowing out of the country to the world's cheapest labor markets. The leading indicator of economic health, the consumer confidence index, bounces like a ping-pong ball. As therapy for stress, we shop; to overcome anxiety, we eat. Do economists realize that our confidence index rises in direct proportion to our absolute lack of real confidence? We, the victims of confidence, accumulate the dead weight of unrecycleable purchases and obesity.

Then there are the warnings against everything that is essential for life on the planet. Nothing is safe – not the air (particulates and asthma are on the rise), not the water (a toxic blend of arsenic and MTBE), and most certainly not our food. Any worries we once attached to pesticide residues on our fruits and vegetables seem now to pale by comparison to recent dramatic warnings against eating more than one monthly serving of salmon (it's laced with dioxin) or two servings of tuna (it's saturated with mercury). And now that we have our first reported cases of mad cow, a hamburger invites a deadly game of Russian roulette. Even an unremarkable garnish like green onions can send hundreds to the hospital with e-coli infections.

Festering uncertainties over food may well have their ramification in our nation's frenetic culture of food fads. The Atkins diet has taken a fat hungry nation by storm. Now we can eat chocolate, the darker the better. Eggs are okay, as well as unlimited meat. Contrariwise, there are the food ascetics such as raw fooders, who view the application of heat to food as corruption; and the calorie restrictors, who practice a lifetime of near starvation for the sake of achieving longevity. By comparison to these more extremist foodways, vegetarianism has become somewhat commonplace. Even the more rigid veganism is hardly noteworthy.

Not to be outdone by the faddists, there are the growing ranks of people who find themselves allergic to certain basic foodstuffs. For some, a peanut – even its aroma – can mean instant death. For others, an oyster can produce anaphylactic shock. Less dramatic, but more pervasive are the numbers of people who see a correlation between diet and a host of chronic symptoms such as gastric distress, headache, shortness of breath, and panic attack. A nation of postmodern hunger artists, we concoct elaborate dietary stratagems to avoid wheat, dairy products, or fruit pectin. We read ingredient labels searching for telltale injurious traces of gluten or whey. We monitor our food intake and police our diets as if control over our bodies might balance against the lack of control over every other sector of our lives. Clearly the balancing act is a mind game whose benefits accrue only so long as the food faddist maintains belief in the fetish properties of enzymes, vitamins, and minerals. To cease to believe is to risk falling prey to our nation's other food culture threat: the wanton consumption of overly abundant salt, sugar, and saturated fat. Portrayed as more dangerous than mad cows and toxic fish, our slide into chronic diabetes raises the haunting specter of amputation, blindness, heart disease, and stroke.

As if pathological worry over food were not enough, we tend to whip ourselves into a frenzy over every new virus that appears on the world's horizon. These we translate into the science-fiction scenario of an isolated unsuspecting population inexplicably victimized by an alien species. Not unlike the attack of the killer bees, West Nile virus is characterized as an invading force waging a state by state campaign across the country. Even though epidemiologists inform us that the advent of new diseases has something to do with world climate change and the dynamics of globalized systems of exchange, we seem unable to break the spell of irrational fear. SARS, influenza and now Avian flu are launched out of Asia and we, the hapless victims, await their onslaught. The scenario of an unexpected and deadly attack functions as a trope for our society's dreaded anticipation of another attack by foreign terrorists. Surprise and helplessness are the lived experience of a society that imagines itself autonomous, cut off from the rest of the world, blissfully adrift in an immaculate sea. But the fear we attach to diseases has less to do with the trope of terror and very much more to do with ruthless neo-conservative economic policies that relegate 44 million Americans to the ranks of the uninsured. Hysteria over new diseases is born of every American's unconscious recognition that access to health care is precarious; compensated time off from work not guaranteed; and the nation's ability to confront the demands of a real epidemic uncertain. Science fiction is the dread of the real.

More frustrating than horrifying is the nation's preoccupation with technology glitches. The pleasurable rush associated with each new technology acquisition is balanced against ever present and mounting dissatisfactions: the anger we feel when the telephone menu doesn't include the option we desperately need, or when a misdirected or miscalculated bill precludes all attempt at arbitration and demands only to be paid, or when our credit card registers denial of payment even though we paid our balance, or when the computer crashes taking everything with it. All these frustrations are trivial by comparison to the dread of identity theft. Here, the media fans our fears with post-Cold War tales of sinister Russian computer hackers who steal credit card numbers by the ream and sell them in wholesale lots of a hundred or a thousand to spree buyers. There are also stories of entire bank accounts reduced to zero in a day by unscrupulous janitors who search bank trash for check stubs. Not gratuitously, identity theft conjures middle-class fears of shady foreigners and underclass or racial others. It also dramatizes the middle-class subject's quandary over disconnection. With face-to-face exchange supplanted by technology (a processes abetted by an economy that would rather invest in technological upgrades than pay workers to perform face-to-face exchanges), we cast our identifying numbers into the void. Preoccupation with identity theft articulates the subject's unwillingness to be subsumed as data.

Of course, all worry that we attach to technology and the economy, health and health care, merely amplifies the main source of our national sense of foreboding: the fear of another terrorist attack. The attack on the Twin Towers broke our charmed sense of invulnerability and isolation. Suddenly, our nation was rent and sundered like every other place on the globe.

While the attack on the Towers was a singular event, which can never be replicated, its facticity begs repetition. Thus, we live in the shadow of inevitability, made all the more dreadful because no one can predict where or when disaster will strike. The CIA, the FBI, the NSA, constitute a babble of misinformation. Assessments sow doubt, as the intelligence community becomes scapegoat for our government's opportunistic war.

We, the denizens of the world's superpower state, experience ourselves as powerless. Nowhere is this more abjectly apparent than when we queue for airport security. Willingly, we strip our outerwear, remove our shoes, and shuffle through metal detectors like dutiful penitents. Some of us even congratulate the security agents for presuming us guilty before the x-rays prove us innocent. We live our nation's awful pre-emptive power with the resigned docility of a herd of cattle. Innuendo and hearsay prevail. Internet "chatter" warns that our bridges or nuclear power stations have been targeted, a cabalistic faith in numerology is cause to cancel certain transatlantic flights, and an inopportune joke sends a French tourist to Rikers Island. Willing to believe the worst and perpetually in a state of low-level panic, we jump to conclusions. Every plane crash, every power blackout is immediately attributed to terrorists. Political forces and the media collude in a campaign of managed fear. Our President, dressed as a fighter pilot, lands on a carrier deck to proclaim the end of major hostilities in Iraq. But subsequent casualties mount as convoys fall prey to improvised explosive devices, the UN mission explodes, and hundreds of Iraqi "collaborators" are targeted. Meanwhile, Rumsfeld blunders on, Powell contradicts his boss, and the Commander in Chief dangles like a puppet on a string at the behest of Cheney and Halliburton. These are the image bites fed to us daily. Is there a win in this picture?

Meanwhile, back on the home front, the newly created Office of Homeland Security promulgates alarm. Rumors sharpen into threats as the color-coded alert system jumps from yellow to orange. Is the office acting on whim or intentionally manipulating the nation's fear? Holidays invariably bring heightened alerts. Is this because the terrorists will be able to kill more of us during heavy travel times? Or is our government taking advantage of family fun to better hold us hostage? The fact that we believe the government capable of manipulating the fear factor merely underscores our sense of powerlessness and uncertainty. The ideology of security that blankets us like a burial shroud gives proof to a repressive state apparatus. Indeed, security is compulsory. Notwithstanding the brave but scattered communities who have rejected the mandates of the USA Patriot Act, the majority of us seem willing to accept arrest without counsel, incarceration without access to habeas corpus, surveillance without court order, and a vast array of data-mining techniques that burrow through our travel itineraries and purchase invoices. Compliant and complacent, we are learning to monitor our behavior. Soon, the airport will be everywhere.

Risk is all but impossible and well-nigh illegal. This is not to deny that everything we do is a risk. Given the numbers of

Americans who die in highway accidents, our daily commute to work is extremely risky. And if the volatility of the stock market is any indication, our investments – indeed many of our pension funds – are a gamble. Moreover, with cancer, heart disease and diabetes popping up in every neighborhood, good health appears to be a question of luck. But we don't live our lives as a gamut of risks. To do so would be to question the very nature of capitalism's priorities. Well-being will never be as profitable as all the things that turn our lives into risky business.

Because the normalcy of daily life is bought with the denial of all the risks we face, it comes as quite a shock when a real risk taker emerges from the numbed and anxious multitude to throw caution to the wind with an act of pure risk. All the commodified and professionalized versions of risk spawned by cable television's ESPN-2 are, by comparison, hollow contrivance. How risky is bungee jumping, demolition derby, or competition skateboarding when seen in the light of Kirk Jones' death-defying plunge over Niagara Falls?

His feat is a miracle – and a parable – for our time. Imagine, of the fifteen people who have stuffed themselves into various protective barrels and plummeted over the falls, only ten have survived. Mr. Jones' feat is all the more astounding because he went over with only the clothes on his back, although many newspaper accounts mention his parka as explanation for his survival. The possibility of anyone surviving such a feat should be gauged against the more than four hundred suicides over the last half-century who climbed over the security barrier, much like Jones, and plummeted "more than 170 feet ... to the deep whirlpools and jagged rocks of the gorge below."[72] Imagine the awestruck bystanders who saw Jones float by (according to one "He was smiling"[73]), then saw him disappear over the brink to emerge unscathed from the roaring torrent.

This is a story worthy of a superhero – an event that begs cinematic digital recreation. But no! Mr. Jones' incredible victory over the falls has been the object of intense public reprimand. A fellow daredevil who twice survived the falls, once "in a barrel wrapped in inner tubes, and in 1995, when he made the plunge with his girlfriend in another makeshift barrel ... said 'Jones' leap cheapens the legend.'"[74] And Roger Woodward (who inadvertently went over the falls as the result of a boating accident and survived primarily because at that time he was seven years old, wearing a life jacket, and floating like a cork) wanted only to distance himself from Jones. As he put it, "I think it's silly foolishness and I don't want to have anything to do with it."[75]

To make matters worse, Jones was arrested as soon as he was fished out of the gorge. Charged with "mischief and unlawfully performing a stunt,"[76] Jones earned the possibility of a $10,000 fine rather than the fame and fortune he sought. Not surprisingly, he began to backtrack on the nature of his stunt. Where his comments once bespoke confidence and pride – he explained that he had previously "scouted the area,"[77] he was sure "there was a spot you could jump and survive,"[78] and he hoped for a place "in the *Guinness Book of World Records*"[79] –

he, instead, began to rationalize his stunt as the desperate act of a man depressed over his family's lost business and his own unemployment. No wonder. The justice of the peace who set his bail "admonished Mr. Jones ... to stay out of Canada except for visits to court."[80] What's more, the head of the Niagara Parks Commission "called the stunt 'stupid' [and complained that Jones' act had put] the fire department, the paramedics, everyone – at risk."[81] Thus risk was reversed and absorbed by the authorities who police risk. Similarly, all the newspaper and television accounts took pains to fold everything miraculous and amazing about the event into a litany of blame, warning, and rebuke. Luckily, Mr. Jones bobbed like a cork upon the tide of public condemnation: word has it he joined "a Texas circus as the world's greatest stunt man;"[82] his advice to us all "When you are feeling down, just remember the power of the Niagara."[83]

Less spectacular, but hazardous nonetheless is Charles McKinley's stunt. Curling his "5ft 8in"[84] frame inside a "3ft by 3ft"[85] cargo crate, Mr. McKinley had himself shipped from New York's JFK Airport to his parent's house in De Soto, Texas. That the stunt was something of a whim is borne out by the fact that no account offers an explanation of why McKinley didn't choose a more orthodox method of transport. He seems simply to have taken advantage of his job as a shipping clerk with an airfreight company to quell a spate of "homesickness"[86] at his employer's expense. Exemplifying Michel De Certeau's notion of "poaching,"[87] wherein office workers use company time and technology for personal pursuits, McKinley billed his boss the $550.00 for his freight.[88]

Like most freight, McKinley followed an indirect itinerary – from the Bronx to Newark; thence to Fort Wayne, Indiana; and on to Dallas-Fort Worth Airport. From there, he was trucked to his parent's home, where the deliveryman "noticed eyes looking at him from between the slats in the cargo crate."[89] Once the lid was removed, McKinley "popped"[90] out, greeted his "stunned"[91] mother, and calmly went inside the house.

In packaging himself like a very ordinary piece of cargo, Mr. McKinley performed the extraordinary. Indeed, he risked his life. If he had not had the good fortune of being transported in a pressurized plane, he most probably would have perished. But was McKinley acclaimed for the novelty and risk of his stunt? Was he invited to tell his tale on the *Tonight Show* with Jay Leno? No, that plum fell to Sergeant Gregory Artesi of the Dallas Sheriff's Department.[92] Not unlike the Niagara daredevil, McKinley was arrested soon after emerging from his crate. He "now faces possible federal stowaway charges."[93] Additionally, his apprehension alerted authorities to outstanding charges for writing bad checks. Once again, the forces of law and order neutralized risk by leveling blame and recrimination on the stuntman.

Curiously, the media, ever eager for a sensational story, did not choose to dramatize the difficulty of McKinley's act. Rather, all accounts seized his prank as an opportunity to fan the flames of terrorist threat. Instead of depicting McKinley as a benign trickster, the press condemned him for revealing security lapses in our air cargo system. "Had he been a trained terrorist with weapons hidden in the crate, McKinley might have been able to commandeer the plane and crash it into a building just as the 9/11 hijackers did."[94] His act summoned hysterical calls "for the arming of cargo pilots,"[95] while the Transportation Security Administration pointed to their "Tiger Teams made up of former CIA and FBI agents and retired members of military special operations units,"[96] as precaution against copy-cat stowaways. Taken aback by the overwhelming negative reaction to his stunt McKinley remarked, "I never thought I'd have a terrorist label on me."[97]

Less risky but somewhat harrowing is the stunt staged by the professional illusionist David Blaine. Suspended in a "seven by seven by three foot"[98] plexiglass box over the Thames, Mr. Blaine performed a 44-day fast. Clearly Blaine selected the site with an eye to history and the development of his career. In performing his stunt adjacent to London's Tower Bridge, Blaine made it clear that he sees himself following in the footsteps of the world's most renowned illusionist, Harry Houdini, who, one hundred years earlier, had himself "handcuffed, sewn in a bag and thrown into the Thames."[99] The master escape artist emerged unscathed to accept the crowd's acclaim.

Mr. Blaine, however, was the object of public scorn. People "hurled eggs, golf balls and paint" at him.[100] Others assailed him with the enticing aromas of "food cooking below."[101] Some bystanders taunted him with "[b]ared breasts and buttocks."[102]

Assured of notoriety, if not fame, Blaine performed his gig to the tune of £1 million put up by "Channel 4 and Sky One TV."[103]

Journalists attributed the carnival of public rebuke occasioned by Blaine's stunt to two primary causes. First of all, as a professional, Blaine was perceived as usurping the hunger strike as a tool of prisoners and the disenfranchised for crass self-aggrandizement. Second, as an American, Blaine became the focus of public anger over "Britain's perceived toadying to the US on Iraq."[104]

Blaine should have taken a cue from Franz Kafka, who not long after Houdini's stunt drafted the tale of "A Hunger Artist." Like Blaine, Kafka's Hunger Artist was a professional faster. At the peak of his career, he was the object of intense public fascination. "[C]hildren stood open-mouthed, holding each other's hands for greater security, marveling at him as he sat there pallid."[105] Sometimes he stretched out "an arm through the bars so that [onlookers] might feel how thin it was."[106] And there were "relays of permanent watchers selected by the public"[107] to make sure the Hunger Artist did not have a hidden stash of food. But times changed. The crowds fell by the wayside and the Hunger Artist was forced to sell himself and his act to a circus. There, he languished in his cage amongst the far more lively animals in the menagerie until one day his ultimate fast claimed his life.

Unlike the Hunger Artist, Mr. Blaine was taken "by ambulance to hospital,"[108] there to be slowly reintroduced to calories. Undoubtedly, he will live to perform other stunts – all of them worthy of the *Guinness Book of World Records*.

The crowds who heckled Blaine translated what the illusionist conceived as pure performance into a properly political act. In recognizing that his stunt too closely paralleled the grim reality of political prisoners, the crowd jeered and taunted to produce the art of political theater. What the crowd may well have sensed is that Blaine, suspended in his plexiglass cell over the metropolis, mimicked the plight of the 650 detainees held in solitary confinement thousands of miles away at Guantanamo's Camp X-Ray. A misnomer if there ever was one, Camp X-Ray's function is to hide rather than reveal. As one lawyer put it, it's "a legal and moral black hole."[109] The direct antithesis of Blaine's public exhibition, the Guantanamo prisoners are held out of sight and well-nigh out of mind. Their cells are not of plexiglass, but "heavy wire mesh."[110] And, unlike Mr. Blaine who is designated a professional, they have no status, not even that of prisoner of war. Finally, where Blaine's performance fits a temporal frame, a 44-day run, the prisoners at Guantanamo are condemned to the temporal limbo of open-ended terms. When Blaine remarked that "he hoped the test would help him find his 'truths'"[111] did he understand that his truth lies elsewhere?

Mr. Blaine's performance stands in metaphoric relationship to the Taliban and Al Qaeda fighters we call "illegal combatants." Blaine and the detainees are comparable in form although vastly dissimilar in detail. The figure that best expresses the simultaneity of metaphoric replication and transformation is that of the asymmetrical clone. If the popular-science conception of cloning conjures the horrifying notion of an endless series of replicants – each one the mirror image of the one that preceded it – the reality of cloning is the expression of difference. Countless environmental factors and the role of mitochondrial DNA combine to make absolute identity an impossibility. While it might have taken a shepherd's trained eye to discern the differences between Dolly the sheep and her mother, most cloned animals from mice to pigs express great variation in detail. Thus, Elsie, cloned from Lady, the last surviving Enderby Island cow, "is the genetic duplicate of Lady, proven by analysis of microsatellite DNA,"[112] but she displays vastly different coat color markings. Where Lady has bands of white encircling her dark body, her clone has only patches. They resemble each other only in so far as any Enderby Island cow might resemble another.

If the trope of the asymmetrical clone provides a means for detecting the metaphoric relationship between a gratuitous performance act conducted in the First World and that same world's dirty secret in Guantanamo, it also supplies the key for revealing the refracted political mirror-images that haunt both the cargo crate and Niagara stuntmen. What most impressed journalists and bystanders alike about Kirk Jones' feat is that he survived Niagara with no more than the shirt on his back. To a culture wedded to technological solutions and habitually armed with all manner of gear, the stuntman's victory over the falls represents the contradictory evidence that simplicity is sometimes the best weapon. By the logic of the asymmetrical clone, Mr. Jones is the displaced embodiment of the 9/11 hijackers, who penetrated airport security and commandeered four passenger jets armed only with box cutters. The stuntman and the hijackers both tested the limits of self-sacrifice. One emerged unscathed from the water's maelstrom. The others were consumed in fiery immolation. Their acts wed formal symmetry to asymmetrical expression.

Similarly, the cargo-crate stuntman is the asymmetrical clone of the thousands of illegal immigrants shipped overland and oversea in containers. The lark that motivated the stuntman is the obverse of the immigrant's dire economic need. The pleasant surprise that greeted the deliveryman and the stuntman's mother in De Soto, Texas is the opposite of the grisly horror that confronted Federal agents at a Texas truck stop, where the bodies of Mexican immigrants were found in an abandoned tractor-trailer. The truth of Mr. McKinley's episode of poaching on the system is the reality of large-scale trafficking in modern-day indentured labor.

Ours is not a culture practiced in the art of taking wondrous, inexplicable events as signs. We have no way to recognize our stuntmen as portents of the real, figures who tap the deep nerves of history to render visible what we repress. Failing to read the truth in metaphor, we fail to live historically. Missed opportunities to see ourselves as the manifestation of the others we deny cycle through the media as disruptive, but wholly trivial events.

We might take instruction in reading metaphorically from anthropologist Michael Taussig whose book *The Devil and Commodity Fetishism* reckons the significance of the world's consummate illusionist: the devil. Contrary to commonly held assumptions about the superhuman powers of the devil, Taussig found that Colombian peasants who harbored devil beliefs, and possibly even made pacts with the devil, did not expect more than "limited goods" in return.[113] What's more, local belief held that wealth gained from the devil "is barren. It cannot serve as productive capital but has to be spent immediately…".[114] The peasants were in dire straits, recently thrown off their lands and reduced to landless wage laborers by the massive capitalist restructuring of agrarian production. Why would they conceive of a devil with such limited capabilities? This is the question that led Taussig to recognize that the peasants held the devil as more than fetish, more, even, than evil deity. They had, indeed, conceptualized the devil as potent metaphor, one capable of signifying the impact of capitalism on their lives "as an evil and destructive way of ordering economic life."[115] The devil was not meant to improve their lives, but to explain their lives. Thus, the devil, an alien figure derived from western religion and apt embodiment of capitalism's profit motive, was adopted by the dispossessed as their means for expressing back to themselves their own alienation. In this instance, the devil is capitalism's asymmetrical clone.

On a lesser, more mundane level our stuntmen signify back to us realities about our world that we either avoid or seek to deny. Ours is a society that chooses not to acknowledge the consequences of our acts in the world. We repress our truths in a blanket of forgetfulness and numbed anxiety. But our efforts to police ourselves are not fully successful. Like the body of a murder victim that – even though shackled – rises to the surface of a lake to bear witness to a crime, the stuntmen rose to the surface of suffocating banality. Serendipitously, all three performed during the same three-month period, October to December 2003. Not coincidentally, we had just commemorated the second anniversary of 9/11. Against the backdrop of orchestrated national remembrance, the stuntmen offered exciting new acts – a regular three-ring circus. Two daredevils and an illusionist – how better to break the pall of sympathy for the dead and renewed evocations of national peril. Little did we know that our entertainers bore witness to the very truths we hope our entertainments will erase.

Fearful, yet comforted in our superpower state, we imagine a world where traumas and dire inequality happen (and are contained) elsewhere. But the globalized world is continuous and its horrors cycle throughout. If our stuntmen are asymmetrical clones of another's horror, they confirm the influence of environmental factors – the privilege and wealth that enable our culture to produce stuntmen where another generates hijackers, destitutes, immigrants, and political detainees. Blind to history and surfeited with entertainments, we are condemned to read portents as no more than wonders.

6

QUIEN ES MAS MACHO?

By the spring of 2004 America was beginning to realize that the war in Iraq had not been won even though the televised narrative of the war emphasized successful closure with two definitive staged events: the toppling of Saddam's grotesquely huge statue in Firdos Square (a much better choreographed event than the extrication of the real Saddam from his spider hole, which only goes to prove the Baudrillardian notion that the virtual is more convincing than the real); and the landing of our jumpsuit-clad President on board the Carrier Abraham Lincoln to proclaim the end of the major hostilities (another virtual event). The insurgency that would ignite a growth industry in kidnappings, beheadings, car bombings, and 'no-go zones' had begun to take shape. Lamely, the administration pinned the blame for discontent on remnant Ba'athists and rogue foreigners. Certainly, no fault could be brought to bear against the occupation with its pro-consul government, America-only no-bid reconstruction contracts, and lucrative jobs for foreign contract workers.

Into the chaos, CBS's *60 Minutes* dropped a bomb that exploded Iraq into America's heartland. Notwithstanding concerted pressure from the Pentagon, the program aired photos depicting obscene and brutal acts of torture conducted by Americans on duty in Iraq's Abu Ghraib prison. Dramatically and irrevocably, the photos put the lie to the myth of America, consecrated throughout our culture, that we are a good-hearted, fine, upstanding, god-fearing, and family loving people who want only to spread the blessings of commerce and democracy to the rest of the world. The photos from Abu Ghraib delivered a body blow to our sanctimonious self-image in a way that news reports of the war's carnage have failed to achieve. We are a sheltered people, largely protected from the dire consequences of our war – not allowed to see the coffins shipped home to Dover, Delaware, rarely brought face to face with the maimed who recuperate in overcrowded VA hospitals, and unwilling to confront the monetary cost of the war – the four billion monthly and the projected $300 to $500 billion overall that will be levied on subsequent generations.

If the rude eruption of blatant torture on our TV screens wasn't enough, the Abu Ghraib photos were most deeply troubling because of the dramatic incongruity that they underscored between young, grinning, white Americans and their abject victims. Fresh-faced American girls who could easily double as Disney employees are shown smiling over a pile of naked prisoners and enthusiastically giving the "thumbs up" while Iraqi men are forced to masturbate or simulate sex. Mind you, this is the country that had a tizzy fit over Janet Jackson's naked breast. How then to explain Lynndie England leading an Iraqi prisoner on a leash?

Slavoj Žižek maintains that the Abu Ghraib photos offer insight into "the obscene underside of US popular culture."[116] The Iraqi prisoners whose images were splashed across our TV screens and front pages "were effectively being initiated into American culture."[117] And Americans who viewed the photos were being instructed in the brutality we daily disavow.

Understandably, the photos hastened a flurry of responses. Right-wing shock jocks laughed them off as good ol' American fun no different than a frat-boy hazing. Taking them more seriously, Congress summoned investigations wherein John McCain famously called for accountability up the chain of command. Meanwhile, Secretary Rumsfeld and a host of military and intelligence officers sought to cast the entire debacle as the fault of a few "bad apples." Not to be outdone, journalist Seymour Hersh published a series of investigative reports in the *New Yorker*[118] that attributed much of the blame for Abu Ghraib to a phantasmagoric special-access-program under the command of the sinister Stephen Cambone (one of Rumsfeld's cohorts) that apparently operates without impunity in America's global war on terror to track, kill, and occasionally extract information.

As with most post-9/11 commentary, the media offered scant response by intellectuals to the Abu Ghraib photos. Žižek's essay appeared in the *London Review of Books*, while Susan Sontag wrote in the *New York Times Magazine* and Jean Baudrillard in *Libération*. In agreement with Žižek, both Sontag and Baudrillard saw the photos as typically American for their union of torture and pornography. And all three affirmed that the most telling photo is not the one of the ice packed corpse, or the naked man cringing in the face of attack dogs, or even the wounded prisoner being stitched up by his tormentors. Rather, all three singled out the image of a man, hooded and robed, shown standing on a box with his outstretched arms in a sustained stress position. From his fingers dangle electric wires. Apparently, the prisoner was told that he'd be electrocuted if he fell off the box or so much as moved his arms. Where the other images capture the obscene vulgarity of torture, this one conveys physical and psychological pain as an aesthetic – the pornographic sublime. According to Žižek, the haunting effect of the photo derives from its "theatrical staging."[119] Commenting that he first took it for "a piece of performance art,"[120] he found the photo summoning up "Robert Mapplethorpe's photographs, [and] scenes from David Lynch movies."[121]

Sontag's assessment of the photo is more complicated because she had access to two versions of the same photo. One version is cropped and shows only the victim as an isolated and thereby aestheticized figure. The other version is uncropped. In it, a fully clothed American man intrudes into the photo's frame, his plump belly girthed with a too-tight belt. At ease, nonchalant, oblivious to the prisoner's distress, he devotes his attention to the camera he holds in his hand, adjusting it for his next shot. Astutely, Sontag, whose work includes essays on holocaust, comments that "snapshots in which executioners placed themselves among their victims are exceedingly rare."[122] The exceptions she notes are "some of the photographs of black victims of lynching taken between the 1880s and 1930s, which show Americans [presumably white], grinning beneath the naked, mutilated body of a black man or woman hanging behind them from a tree."[123]

Baudrillard's apprehension of the photo is the most complicated. Calling it "phantasmagoric"[124] for its reversibility, he sees the prisoner threatened with electrocution as a body become emblematic of the hood he wears. Symbolically, he reckons the victim an apparition of the Ku Klux Klan, seen here in obverse – something of a photographic negative where the robe is black unlike the Klansman's white. But more than simply giving us a negative of the Klan, reversibility alludes to the unexpected and cunning way that this highly aestheticized image conjoins victim and executioner. Indeed, Baudrillard sees the figure as doubly reversible when he reads the iconography of crucifixion in the prisoner's outstretched arms.

Famous for symbolic intuition, Baudrillard does not belabor his insight by attempting to fathom the double incongruity of a Muslim who figures Christ and a victim of lynching who embodies the Klan. As a European, Baudrillard may not feel obliged to reckon the contradictions of our history in his interpretation. Suffice it to say that in overleaping historical specificity, he reads the figure as a sign. If we, then, read history back into the sign, we are in a position to grasp the image as an icon that conflates the history we repress (lynching) with the history we disavow (torture).

Klan and cross, emblem of vigilante white Protestantism – is this not now the brand that marks our cowboy President's holy war? Does the Invisible Empire of the Klan that D.W. Griffith portrayed in heroic terms one hundred years ago in his famously scandalous film *Birth of a Nation*, now infuse our not so invisible empire, famously extolled by right-wing ideologues? Can we say that the particular sentiments of fearful hate and inferiority that found expression in the Klan have ever been resolved? Can we say that the social factors of ignorance and poverty that fueled the Klan's growth have ever been overcome? Resilient, the Klan has undergone a number of incarnations since its inception in the nineteenth century. Malleable, the Klan has shaped itself in response to prevailing histories. But no matter its moment or guise, the Klan has always only stood for the supremacy of white Protestant men. "One hundred percent American," this is how the Klan represents itself. At this point in history, when the KKK itself is an abeyance, allied with neo-fascist and Christian identity sects, might we not say that its ethos has expanded well beyond the actual Klan to permeate our nation's foreign policy? Do the Abu Ghraib photos demonstrate that the Klan is us?

Born in the aftermath of America's Civil War, the KKK rallied defeated white soldiers and organized them in a secret vigilante terrorist network. It preached the resurgence of white supremacy against the inroads of victorious northern reformers dubbed "scalawags" and the newly freed blacks perceived to be riding on their coat tails. Is it remarkable or merely historical that insurgents in Iraq have rallied for similar reasons and honed the same tactics? Can we reverse the photo of the prisoner threatened with electrocution and see him in obverse – no longer the victim, but now the hooded and robed Al Zarqawi. As his clan's supreme executioner, Al Zarqawi also dons hood and robe. He, too, puts himself in the picture, seen behind a kneeling westerner soon to be beheaded – all of it broadcast for worldwide consumption on Al-Jazeera.

Kidnapping, rape, and torture were the American Klan's methods; the preservation of white womanhood its rationale. In Iraq, our acts of torture and our perceived defilement of holy sites and Muslim women have unleashed a mirror image of our Klan that, then, rains terror upon us – kidnappings, beheadings, and bombings leveled at foreign scalawags (the contractors, journalists, and military personnel) and all those Iraqi policemen and soldiers perceived to be riding on our coat tails. If the Klan has been born more than once, has it not now mutated into twin forms, American and Iraqi, the double strands of a terrorist DNA?

The first manifestation of the Klan lasted less than a decade. Never well organized in the first place, it quickly fell into a chaotic assemblage of gangs and was disbanded by its Grand Wizard in 1870. But it was reborn with a vengeance in the 1920s, this time not in the South, but in the heartland of America's Midwest; and not amongst the most destitute, but in the middle classes. Indeed, as Kathleen Blee puts it, the Klan gave expression to the very same "ideas and values that shaped white Protestant life in the early twentieth century."[125] This means it was nativist, xenophobic, and masculinist. As its founder, William J. Simmons, described it, the Klan was a fraternity for "real American masculinity"[126] – words hauntingly similar to the present-day slogan for the United States Marine Corps. Isn't masculinity at the crux of America's military? Surely the policy towards homosexuals – the infamous "don't ask, don't tell" – suggests that less than perfect men have to be closeted. As for women in the military male fraternity, the 1920s Klan supplies a solution in its Katechism: "The Klan believes in the purity of womanhood and the fullest measure of freedom compatible with the highest type of womanhood including the suffrage."[127] The Klan opened its ranks to include women in the separate but equal Women's Ku Klux Klan. In contrast, today's post-Civil Rights abolition of Jim Crow stipulates that women would have to be brought into the ranks without distinction. Worries over an impending reinstatement of the draft are often laid to rest when it's pointed out that the military would be fully co-ed, like a college dorm.

If the KKK is apt comparison to the military, it warrants pointing out that the 1920s Klan collapsed of its own contradictions best summarized in the downfall of D.C. Stephenson, leader of the Indiana Klan. Exemplary of what it means to be a "one hundred percent American man," Stephenson amassed power with an eye toward political office outside the Klan. Preaching Christian values, but leading a life of debauchery, he was eventually convicted of kidnapping, torturing, mutilating, and causing the suicide of a young female social worker. Possibly taking Stephenson's debacle as object lesson, today's Klan has reversed its previous position on women. Much like the Promise Keepers, the current Klan "affirms traditional gender roles as the only correct ones for God-fearing Christians ... And denounces affirmative action programs on the grounds that these curb the rights of white men."[128]

In raising the apparition of the Klan, I don't mean to imply that the American soldiers who tortured Iraqis in Abu Ghraib prison were card-carrying members of the KKK (although coincidentally they were all white and southern). Rather, the ghostly image of the Klan that haunts the photo of the hooded victim of simulated electrocution signals that all the photos should be read as documents of lynching. Recall the crucified aspect of the victim and bear in mind that the Klan "wielded religion as a weapon of terror and political power."[129] Indeed, it saw itself as "the masculine arm of Protestantism."[130] How starkly the symbolic crucifixion of the Iraqi conflates his Christian persecutors with the very terrorists we pursue. These also use religion as a tool of terror to proclaim themselves the avenging masculine arm of their religion, Islam.

As documents of lynching, the photos suggest that the values of the KKK saturate our military. How, then, to account for the high percentage of non-white personnel in the military who as individuals cannot expect to reap the benefits that accrue to their white counterparts? Our all-volunteer Army may placate middle-class fears of a reinstituted draft, but it is severely challenged by the economic necessity that underscores volunteerism. Like Jessica Lynch, who joined the Army because she wanted to save for college and couldn't get a job at Wal-Mart, whites with limited economic prospects are ripe for military recruiters as are the Hispanics, Indians, and African Americans, whose representation in the military far exceeds their representation in society as a whole. As America, and most especially its military, becomes the embodiment of multi-culturalism, the category of the scapegoated and racialized "other" we fear, the "other" who threatens our supremacy, the "other" who disturbs us sexually is now the Muslim.

"Do you really think a group of kids from rural Virginia decided to do this on their own?"[131] This is how the lawyer representing one of the "bad apples" raised the question that surely more worldly, better educated principals farther up the military chain of command would have best known how to humiliate a Muslim prisoner. It may well be that neo-conservative ideologues in the Pentagon sketched the ground rules for the systematic torture of Iraqi prisoners. Seymour

Hersh argues convincingly that high-ranking civilian and military personnel – from Secretary Rumsfeld, to General Miller (mastermind of Guantanamo), and on to General Sanchez in Baghdad – all signed off on the orders that set aside many of the Geneva Conventions on the treatment of military prisoners. Famously, Rumsfeld stated that as he typically stands for eight to ten hours a day, he couldn't imagine that maintaining a stress position for two to four hours would constitute torture. In any case, it's abundantly clear that legal briefs prepared by Alberto Gonzales, the President's counsel and nominee for Attorney General, maintain the impunity of the Commander in Chief when it comes to the treatment of so-called "illegal combatants." But all this is not to argue a resurgence of the KKK or to suggest that the Klan has taken over the White House. Nevertheless, all the forces that once found expression in the Klan are now amply accommodated in the cowboy, Born Again religiosity of our President, who initially described our war as a crusade and presides over a vigilante foreign policy. Indeed, the notion of America's supremacist Manifest Destiny, articulated a century ago in terms of a soft voice and a big stick, has been updated into the twenty-first century with the no-holds-barred right to wage pre-emptive war armed with "hell fire" missiles.

And what of Megan, Sabrina, and Lynndie? Where are they in this picture? Smiling, giving the "thumbs up," and in one instance leading a prisoner on a leash; are they like the Klanswomen, willing helpmates of their male counterparts? Or were they, like one Midwesterner put it, just plain "bored …

To, one, do these things, and, two, to take photos"?[132] Like many American youth languishing in dead-end jobs (many of them performed at night like these soldier's shift in the prison) did they tire of their video games and decide to commit some real mayhem? Lynndie England's personal motivations were certainly more complicated. Impregnated by one of her co-defendants, she is living testimony to all the ways women compete with, conform to, and get caught by male-defined models of behavior. Did she and her female cohorts feel pressured to do or outdo what the men were doing? Or did they simply get carried away like a victim of date rape at a frat party? Or maybe they liked degrading men – humiliating them by watching their forced masturbation and gleefully reporting, "he's getting hard,"[133] even though an Iraqi man must be a poor stand-in for the men who really wield power. Or is the Iraqi a poor stand-in? Remember all the western women who fantasized sex with bin Laden? Might the women in the photos be playing their "po' Southern white boy" cohorts against forbidden mysterious "others"?

The answers we might give to the questions are as deficient as the questions themselves. This is because the women figure more than their individual meanings and motivations. On a level larger than themselves, they mobilize the category of white womanhood, which has been at the crux of our history certainly since slavery, and most probably since the Pilgrims first encountered the original Americans. Pure, vulnerable, and ever in need of protection, white womanhood has provided rationale for centuries of male-dominated white supremacist politics. Witness the Jessica Lynch story, packaged for US consumption as a melodrama. It features a young, blond, Southern white girl, trying bravely to do a man's job in a man's army. Sadly, and horrifically, she is captured by lawless and lust-crazed Iraqis. Then, mercilessly, she is tortured – arms and legs broken; and, as a final act of degradation, she is raped anally. This is the tale that seeped into America's newspapers during our Army's initial push from Kuwait into Iraq. How better to rally the nation, let the homefront know what's at stake. Luckily, there's a happy ending. The captive is rescued – and not because Iraqi doctors and nurses did what they could to keep her alive (although they did), and not because her caregivers found a way to let the Americans know of her whereabouts (although they did), but only because valiant US soldiers came to her rescue, video camera in hand to immortalize their exploits. Propaganda may not be terribly inventive, but there could not have been a better opening salvo than this tried and true tale of imperiled white womanhood.

In contrast, the women in the Abu Ghraib photos are shown to be compliant with torture. They are the aiders and abettors – maybe even the instigators – of humiliating and violent acts. But to the extent that they conjure white womanhood (and they cannot help but do so given the embeddedness of racism in our history), they also embody the vulnerable homefront. As such they represent an innocent and victimized America, not a belligerent, warmonger nation. And they summon up everything that Lillian Gish symbolized almost a century ago when, in *Birth of a Nation*, she cowered alone and defenseless in a cabin besieged by a crazed gang of lust-driven blacks (the ur-text for the Jessica Lynch rescue). In *Hooded Americanism*, David Chalmers describes Griffith's staging of imperiled white womanhood and its effects on the movie's audience:

> The tension became unbearable. An orchestral passage from Die Walküre heralded the assembling of the Klansmen. A bugle blast from the pit brought the audience shouting to its feet as the hooded horsemen rode to the rescue. The orchestra matched passages from "The Hall of the Mountain King" to the galloping of the horses' hoofs, as the scene shifted back and forth between the approaching Klansmen and the pale heroine in the cabin surrounded by frenzied blacks.[134]

Today, the media has spawned another version of imperiled white womanhood – the "security mom." Where the early twentieth century imagined a widowed or virgin white woman alone in her cabin or the charred remains of the ancestral manse, we, at the height of the 2004 election campaign, conjure the plight of white suburban moms who, notwithstanding their husbands or the obvious comfort of their lives (clean, well-dressed kids, pleasant neighborhoods with well-tended playgrounds and schools, newish often large cars), still profess an overriding, deep-seated, and persistent fear for their security. Not surprisingly, they are predominantly depicted in support of George Bush, whose wanton decision to wage war is construed as rescue – with or without the Wagnerism overtones. That the "security mom" is an ideological construct is apparent in the fact that no woman of color is ever shown testifying to a near debilitating fear of terrorist attack, nor do the "security moms" ever mention any of the real reasons why a mother might, indeed, feel anxiety in America such as precarious household economics, sky rocketing health care and education costs, rampant domestic gun violence, and a food industry reaping profits on childhood obesity.

If reading the Abu Ghraib photos as examples of lynching reveals white womanhood, preserved from the nineteenth century to the present in the formaldehyde of ideology, what are we to make of the women in the photos when we read them as examples of pornography? – And pornography they surely are if only because each had to be repixilated for American distribution so as to erase the prisoners' genitals in the same way that Janet Jackson's offending breast was repixilated into a suggestive, but indistinct blur. Apparently, only those who preside over American values – people like Donald Rumsfeld and Michael Powell, czar of the FCC – were allowed to see the undoctored photos, much like the members of the Meese Commission who waded through reams of pornography in order to determine just what needed to be censored. We who consumed the televised and newsprint versions of the Abu Ghraib photos were left to fantasize the proscribed body parts. But, then, as Laura Kipnis, author of *Bound and Gagged*, puts it, "pornography is a fantasy form."[135] Do the censors realize that those of us in fear – or awe – of Arab men (as we once were of black men) are apt to fantasize extraordinarily large penises in the space of the redigitized blur?

To Kipnis' dictum, I would add that pornography is also a destabilizing form. In commenting on the transgressive aspect of pornography, Kipnis reasons:

> transgression is no simple thing: it's a precisely calculated endeavor. It means knowing the culture inside out, discerning its secret shames and grubby secrets, and knowing how to best humiliate it …[136]

Those farther up the military chain of command who most probably coached the soldiers in how best to humiliate Arab prisoners knew the taboos that Muslim culture ascribes to nakedness; and, most particularly, homosexuality. Much like the producers of a low-budget porn flick, they set the stage for a sadistic theater. Borrowing from film noir, the producers aimed to use the photos for blackmail. The Iraqis would be turned into compliant spies, intimidated by the threat that the shameful photos would be made public. The script called for the Americans, both male and female, to assume the roles of heterosexuals. After all, power is straight. The Iraqis would play at being homosexuals. They would be forced to masturbate, display their erections to the Americans, and simulate sex with each other.

But this scenario, clearly calculated to transgress and humiliate, spins out of control once we factor in the female protagonists and ask the question: who's looking at whom? As Americans, the women are necessarily scripted as heterosexuals. As such, their parts are limited to the traditional categories of pet or prize. Occasionally they may perform a more risqué role – that of dominatrix – but this, too, conforms with dominant male heterosexual codes.

But who dominants the women's fantasies? They may be looking at the camera, but who are they thinking about? Who elicits their "thumbs up"? And who is "getting hard"? – The clothed American men? Or the naked Iraqis?

And, for that matter, who captivates the American men? – Certainly not the uniformed women. As a fantasy form, pornography makes use of genres and genre expectations, but it doesn't necessarily stick to the script.

What's more, pornography deploys a lot of unwieldy subtexts. Think of all the sexual fantasies and cultural uncertainties that the war has generated. It turns out that what first ignited Falluja is the fact that American soldiers occupied rooftop vantage points, making it possible for them to peer into household courtyards, the only place out-of-doors where Iraqi women may move freely and uncovered. This vignette is more than emblematic of cross-cultural misunderstanding as it lays bare sexual taboos. In a war that pits two different constructions of masculinity against each other, which is the most macho? – The Arab who controls his women, keeps them in their place and dictates how they will act and appear in public? Or the American whose women do what they will, wear pants, drive trucks, and carry guns?

So, in depicting male and female soldiers as partners in crime, do the Abu Ghraib photos represent the height of women's equality with men? Or are the photos documents of white male inferiority and anti-feminist backlash? How better to get back at uppity women than to give them just what they want – black meat. How better to get at the black brute than to taunt him with a woman he can't have.

Just as pornography exceeds its script, so too does it fail to control its audience and its reception. If the intended recipients of the photos as blackmail were the prisoners' family members or employers, the audience of the photos as a porn show were the enlistees (predominantly male), who received and circulated the photos on digital discs. If, in the pornographic underground, the object of everyone's gaze is the hard Iraqi penis, then who is the most macho?

Following Baudrillard's line of argument, we might extend the reversibility of the photos to include the pornographic dimension. Thus, the photos that were intended to transgress Muslim sexual taboos (which they certainly do), also boomerang back upon the perpetrators to transgress the dominant culture's "grubby secrets" – our twin phobias, miscegenation and homo-sexuality. As surely as the Abu Ghraib porn photos humiliate the captives, so too, do they mobilize unintended subtexts wherein white womanhood is tempted by the non-white "other" and the manly military confronts the homoeroticism inherent in its own homosocial environment.

Back on the homefront where mainstream American culture is carefully sanitized, many Americans who knew of the photos found ways not to have to see them. Unlike the *New York Times*

Magazine which proclaimed "The Photographs Are Us,"[137] they found the obscenity, if not the violence, decidedly un-American. For us, pornography is the XXX video store on the edge of town or the newsstand "girlie" magazine hidden under the counter where women and children won't be shocked by its cover illustration. Even John Ashcroft, our erstwhile Attorney General, whose job it was to arbitrate decency, deemed it necessary to shroud the statue of Justice in his office because he found her sculpted attire too revealing. But pornography cannot be fully suppressed, and not only because the First Amendment guarantees freedom of expression. Indeed, pornography haunts us, most probably because it is so proscribed. Just click on Whitehouse.com and you'll see things George Bush would have to attribute to the devil. Actually, the internet is rife with porn. According to one researcher, "it's the World Wide Web's major economic success"[138] with revenues over $50 million annually.[139] What's more, most internet porn is produced by amateurs, sometimes husband and wife teams. What better way to promote small business and America's entrepreneurial spirit? Then, too, there's e-mail and all that delicious spam. What a surprise to come across ads for an herbal penis enlargement remedy featuring disheartening "before" and stunning "after" photos.

Besides explicit versions, pornography also materializes in ways that most consumers of culture would never recognize. Here, I don't have in mind the host of TV programs with wicked premises – a wealthy bachelor trolling for a mate, a reality show that offers possibilities for wife swapping, not even the metrosexual Fab Five's makeover of a straight and hopelessly clueless guy. These flirt with sexuality but don't have the punch of porn.

According to Kipnis, "Pornography grabs us and doesn't let go."[140] How better to characterize CBS's smash hit *CSI* (*Crime Scene Investigation*), so popular that the original program set in Las Vegas has spawned two prime time clones set in Miami and New York. The show offers the fascinating investigative detail of a Sherlock Holmes mystery catapulted into the high-tech present where the science of forensics has replaced Holmes' deductive reasoning. In a real world beset by uncertainty, *CSI* offers definitive proof of guilt or innocence in the distillation of body fluids, the microscopic analysis of fibers, computerized finger print matching, and, most especially, trace DNA evidence. But the punch of the show derives from something more than the transformation of geek science into crime drama. Indeed, *CSI* is pornography displaced into forensics. The viewer gets weekly doses of pubic hairs, semen soaked sheets, and rape inflicted vaginal scars – all on network TV. What's more, every program is guaranteed to deliver at least one scantly draped body, inert as if in repose, awaiting the inquiring eyes and hands of the examiners. Autopsy is pornography in metaphor. And, it's hard core. *CSI* doesn't stop with a carefully staged pose – a body languid on a bed; or, for those more prurient tastes, draped over a toilet. Nor does it linger on the body's surface with its telltale hairs and fluids. No, just like *Hustler* it plunges in. And it goes even further to open the body in unexpected places, probing it more deeply than Masters and Johnson ever achieved with their probe mounted vaginal camera. With the help of computerized animation, *CSI* visualizes the path of a bullet as it penetrates flesh and organs. Is this not the ultimate fuck? Too bad the body's dead. But, then, so too were some of the prisoners photographed in Abu Ghraib. The soldiers smiling over an ice packed corpse; us at home absorbed by the necrophilia of *CSI* – aren't we all just getting off?

What goes around comes around. The circulation of the Abu Ghraib photos cycles through the pornography of death and brings us back where we began – with lynching. Not invented by the Klan (posses in the West strung up cattle thieves; armies in the Civil War did likewise with deserters), lynching has never been conveniently relegated to the margins of society like a XXX video store, not in the heyday of the Klan and not now with Abu Ghraib. Nor can lynching be construed as the perverted act of a few "bad apples." Newspaper accounts of lynchings conducted in the '20s and '30s invariably report all the "best people" in attendance. Isn't this the way we as a nation like to think of our fighting men and women?

The soldiers at Abu Ghraib used their digital cameras to document themselves in their acts. Performance turned into cultural artifact, they, then, sent their photos to friends, even family members. So too, did photographers in the '20s and '30s document townspeople in their acts of lynching. They made their photos available for purchase – often as postcards which the townspeople sent to their friends and family. Aunt Myrtle who sent her postcard of a sixteen-year-old black boy hanging from a tree to her family with the note: "give this to Bud,"[141] we who received our Abu Ghraib photos via CBS – don't we all share in the popular culture of lynching?

What about Joe who sent his mother a postcard showing the charred and mutilated body of Jesse Washington strung up over the assembled townspeople: "This is the barbeque we had last night. My picture is to the left with a cross over it, your sone [sic] Joe."[142]

And what about the mother of a marine in Iraq who sketched her son's story to me in half sentences and innuendo. He was not wounded; but, then, not quite right. He was sent home. No, not discharged – just in need of rest. Has trouble sleeping; doesn't talk much. The only thing he seemed keen to do was to show his mother his photos of Iraq. There amongst the tourist shots were other photos – his buddies, bare assed and defecating in Iraqi buildings, possibly houses. He wanted his mother to see them. And she wanted me to know. The pornography of war – who really is mas macho?

NOTES

1 November 3 Radio Address.

2 *Greensboro News Record*, December 13, 2001, p. B1.

3 *USA Today*, November 6, 2001, p. A01.

4 *New York Times*, October 15, 2001, p. B8.

5 *Automotive News*, October 29, 2001, p. 51.

6 *New York Times*, October 22, 2001, p. B6.

7 *Bulletin of the Atomic Scientists*, July/August 1999, Vol. 55, No. 4, pp. 7–13.

8 *Ibid.*

9 *USA Today*, November 6, 2001, p. A01.

10 *London Review of Books*, November 29, 2001, p. 26.

11 *Herald Sun*, December 22, 2001, p. A6.

12 *London Review of Books*, November 29, 2001, p. 27.

13 *New York Times*, November 2, 2001, p. B8.

14 *USA Today*, November 6, 2001, p. A01.

15 *Herald Sun*, December 22, 2001 p. A6.

16 Guy Debord, *Society of the Spectacle* (Detroit: Black and Red, 1977), thesis 70.

17 *Ibid.*, thesis 147.

18 Jean Baudrillard, *Selected Writings*, ed. Mark Poster (Cambridge: Polity Press, 1988), p. 172.

19 *New York Times*, October 25, 2002, p. A22.

20 Jean Baudrillard, *The Spirit of Terrorism* (London and New York: Verso, 2002), p. 9.

21 *USA Today*, October 24, 2002, p. 3A.

22 Karl Marx, *The 18th Brumaire of Louis Bonaparte* (New York: International Publishers, 1984), p. 124.

23 *New York Times*, November 10, 2002, p. wk3.

24 Marx, *op. cit.*, p. 124.

25 Jean-Paul Sartre, *Being and Nothingness* (New York: Simon and Schuster, 1973), p. 542.

26 Marx, *op. cit.*, p. 124.

27 Jean Baudrillard, *La Guerra du Golfe N'a Pas Eu Lieu* (Paris: Galileé, 1991), p. 7.

28   Catherine Lutz, *Homefront* (Boston: Beacon Press, 2001), p. 255.

29   1991 Union Calendar No. 228, 105th Congress, 1st Session House Report, "Background."

30   *Ibid.*, p. 120.

31   Anthony Wilden, *The Language of the Self* (Baltimore: Johns Hopkins University Press, 1968), p. 236.

32   Jean Baudrillard, *The Spirit of Terrorism* (London and New York: Verso, 2002), pp. 6–7.

33   Jean-Paul Sartre, *L'Idiot de la Famille* (Paris: Gallimard, 1971), p. 7.

34   *Ibid.*

35   *The Hegel Reader*, ed. Stephen Houlgate (Oxford: Blackwell, 1999), p. 410.

36   *Ibid.*, p. 413.

37   *New York Times*, October 24, 2002, p. A26.

38   *New York Times*, October 26, 2002, p. A31.

39   *Washington Post*, November 4–10, 2002, p. 10.

40   Jean Baudrillard, *The Spirit of Terrorism* (London and New York: Verso, 2002), p. 19.

41   *Ibid.*

42   *New York Times*, October 25, 2002, p. A23.

43   "Osama's Got Mail," *Washington Post*, September 28, 2002, p. C3.

44 Slavoj Žižek, *Welcome to the Desert of the Real* (London and New York: Verso, 2002), p. 19.

45 *Ibid.*, p. 31.

46 *Ibid.*, p. 32.

47 *Ibid.*

48 "Secret of the US Nuclear Bunkers," *Guardian Unlimited*, March 2, 2002.

49 *Ibid.*

50 *Ibid.*

51 *Ibid.*

52 "Notes from the Underground," *Village Voice*, New York, March 19, 2002.

53 "Shadow Government is at Work in Secret," *Washington Post*, March 1, 2002.

54 Žižek, *op. cit.*, p. 9.

55 "Congress Not Advised of Shadow Government," *Washington Post*, March 2, 2002.

56 Jacques Lacan, *Le Désir et son Interprétation* (Paris: Editions de l'Association Freudienne Internationale, 2000), p. 286.

57 "Read This, Then Go Back Up Your Data," *Fortune*, Winter 2002.

58 "Letter from the Chairman," www.national-underground. com, March 3, 2003.

59 "Butler County Hole in the Wall Becomes Acquisition Target," *Post–Gazette*, June 12, 1998.

60 "History Goes Underground," *Presentations*, August 2001.

61 Walter Benjamin, "The Work of Art in the Age of Mechanical Reproduction," in *Illuminations*, ed. Hannah Arendt (New York: Schocken, 1969), p. 221.

62 *Ibid*.

63 *The Dialogues of Plato*, tr. B. Jowett (New York: Random House, 1937), p. 772.

64 *Ibid*.

65 www.iai.co.il, "Products & Services."

66 "Play Fighting," *Wall Street Journal*, February 26, 2002, p. A1.

67 "Tragedy Infiltrates a Bragg Tradition," *Washington Post*, March 3, 2002, p. A03.

68 "Play Fighting," *op. cit*.

69 *Ibid*.

70 *Ibid*.

71 Žižek, *op. cit*., p. 38.

72 "'Happy to be Alive,' Survivor of Falls Plunge is Released," *New York Times*, October 24, 2003, p. B9.

73 "Niagara Falls Survivor: Stunt was 'Impulsive'," CNN.com, October 22, 2003.

74 *Ibid*.

75 "Family Stunned After Son Takes Niagara Falls Plunge and Lives," *New York Times*, October 22, 2003, p. B1.

76 "'My Full Intent to End My Life at Those Falls,' Man Who Plunged Over Niagara Grateful for a Second Chance," *Edmonton Journal*, October 23, 2003, p. A9.

77 "Family Stunned After Son Takes Niagara Falls Plunge and Lives," *op. cit.*

78 "Michigan Man Who Survived Plunge Over Niagara Falls Calls it 'Impulsive Act'," *Canadian Press Newswire*, October 22, 2003.

79 "'My Full Intent to End My Life at Those Falls'," *op. cit.*

80 "'Happy to be Alive'," *op. cit.*

81 "Niagara Falls Survivor: Stunt was 'Impulsive'," *op. cit.*

82 "Niagara Falls Survivor Due in Court," *Associated Press State and Local Wire*, December 18, 2003.

83 "'My Full Intent was to End My Life at Those Falls'," *op. cit.*

84 "Cargo Crate Stowaway Exposes US Security Gap," *Times* (London), September 11, 2003, Overseas News, p. 20.

85 *Ibid.*

86 *Ibid.*

87 Michel De Certeau, *The Practice of Everyday Life* (Berkeley: University of California Press, 1984).

88 "Air Cargo Stowaway Shows Security Lapse," *USA Today*, September 10, 2003 p. B1.

89   *Ibid*.

90   "Odds and Ends," *Associated Press*, September 9, 2003.

91   "Cargo Crate Stowaway Exposes US Security Gap," *op. cit*.

92   "Media Frenzy Follows Stowaway Flier," *Houston Chronicle*, September 14, 2003 p. A34.

93   "Cargo Crate Stowaway Exposes US Security Gap," *op. cit*.

94   "Man Who Shipped Himself Aboard Cargo Plane Exposes Gaps in Security," *Associated Press*, September 10, 2003.

95   *Ibid*.

96   "Air Cargo Stowaway Shows Security Lapse," *op. cit*.

97   "Cargo Crate Stowaway Exposes US Security Gap," *op. cit*.

98   "Taking the Blaine," *Irish Times*, October 11, 2003, p. 51.

99   *Ibid*.

100   *Ibid*.

101   *Ibid*.

102   *Ibid*.

103   *Ibid*.

104   *Ibid*.

105   Franz Kafka, "A Hunger Artist," in *The Penal Colony* (New York: Schocken, 1970), p. 244.

106   *Ibid*.

107   *Ibid*.

108 "Day 44 – Blaine Emerges," www.channel4.com, October 28, 2003.

109 "Australian at Guantanamo in 'Legal and Moral Black Hole,' Lawyer Says," *Washington Post*, December 15, 2003, p. A20.

110 "Guantanamo Bay: A First Hand View of Camp X-Ray," *Federal News Service*, December 18, 2003.

111 "Magician David Blaine Nears End of Hungry London Vigil," *Associated Press*, October 17, 2003.

112 Marie A. Di Berardino, "Animal Cloning: The Route to New Genomics in Agriculture and Medicine," *Differentiation*, 2001, p. 78.

113 Michael Taussig, *The Devil and Commodity Fetishism* (Chapel Hill: UNC Press, 1980), pp. 13–18.

114 *Ibid.*, p. 94.

115 *Ibid.*, p. 17.

116 Slavoj Žižek, "Between Two Deaths," *London Review of Books*, June 3, 2004, p. 19.

117 *Ibid.*

118 Seymour M. Hersh, "Torture at Abu Ghraib," *New Yorker*, May 10, 2004, pp. 42–47. "Chain of Command," *New Yorker*, May 17, 2004, pp. 38–43. "The Gray Zone," *New Yorker*, May 24, 2004, pp. 38–44.

119 Slavoj Žižek, "Between Two Deaths," p. 19.

120 *Ibid.*

121 *Ibid.*

122 Susan Sontag, "Regarding the Torture of Others," *New York Times Magazine*, May 23, 2004, p. 27.

123 *Ibid.*

124 Jean Baudrillard, "Pornographie de la Guerre," *Libération*, May 19, 2004, p.

125 Kathleen Blee, *Women of the Klan* (Berkeley: University of California Press, 1991), p. 17.

126 *Ibid.*, p. 19.

127 *Ibid.*, p. 49.

128 *Ibid.*, p. 176.

129 *Ibid.*, p. 45

130 *Ibid.*

131 Seymour Hersh, *Chain of Command* (New York: Harper Collins, 2004) p. 38.

132 Sasha Abramsky, "Supporting the Troops, Doubting the War," *Nation*, October 4, 2004, p. 14.

133 Hersh, *op. cit.*, p. 24.

134 David Chalmers, *Hooded Americanism, The History of the Ku Klux Klan* (Durham: Duke University Press, 1987) p. 26.

135 Kipnis, Laura, *Bound and Gagged* (Durham: Duke University Press, 1999), p. 69.

136 *Ibid.*, p. 164

137 *New York Times Magazine*, May 23, 2004, title page.

138   Frederick S. Lane, *Obscene Profits, The Entrepreneurs of Pornography in the Cyber Age* (New York: Routledge, 2000), p. 34.

139   *Ibid.*, p. 115.

140   Kipnis, *op. cit.* p. 161.

141   James Allen, Hilton Als, Congressman John Lewis and Leon F. Litwack, *Without Sanctuary: Lynching Photography in America* (Santa Fe: Twin Palms, 2000), Plates 54, 55.

142   *Ibid.*, Plates 25, 26.